THE BACKPACKER'S BUDGET FOOD BOOK

❊

How to Select and Prepare
Your Provisions from
Supermarket Shelves

FRED POWLEDGE

David McKay Company, Inc.

NEW YORK

To Naomi Morrison

Library of Congress Cataloging in Publication Data

Powledge, Fred.
  The backpacker's budget food book.

  Includes index.
  1. Outdoor cookery.   2. Backpacking.
I. Title.
TX823.P68   641.5'78   77-21342
ISBN 0-679-50809-0 pbk.

10 9 8 7 6 5 4 3 2 1

MANUFACTURED IN THE UNITED STATES OF AMERICA

CONTENTS

1

INVITATION
TO ENJOYMENT

This book is intended to be a cooking guide for the recreational backpacker, and one that demonstrates how any interested trail traveler can assemble lightweight, nutritious, appetizing meals largely from standard grocery-store sources.

I say "cooking guide" because I want the book to be more than just a collection of recipes useful to backpackers, ski-tourers, snowshoers, canoeists, sailors, hunters, fishers, and others who like to get away from pavement and bureaucracy. I hope the reader will be able to use the guide to build her or his own *system* of outdoors cooking, just as I have built mine over the past several years of walking and eating in the woods. What is presented here is the system that works for me.

I hope no one interprets my suggestions and recommendations as efforts to impose my system on others. One of the greatest things about backpacking is that it simply cannot be done by any rigid formula (although in backpacking, as in any other human endeavor, there are some—the "outdoors leadership" and "survival" people come to mind—who would love to move in and establish strict rules and take all the serendipitous fun away).

I also use the term "recreational backpacker."
I'm being redundant, you may say: Backpacking *is*
recreational, by definition. What I mean is that these
recipes and suggestions are aimed mostly at the
backpacker who takes to the woods for the fun and
joy and peace of it rather than in order to prove
something.

The traveler who needs and wants to prove something—that he or she can get to the tops of all the
mountains above a certain height; that the Appalachian Trail can be traveled in two and a half weeks
—is, in my estimation, almost certainly going to be
so wrapped up in *those* challenges that there will be
little or no interest in the challenge that lies at the
foundation of this book: the invitation to produce
healthy, tasty, and filling, but also extremely lightweight, meals in the woods. The competitive backpacker wants calories, fats, and protein, and in his
drive to lighten his load he usually will have to forgo
some of the more pleasant side effects of face-
stuffing—notably taste and texture. The recreational
backpacker, according to my definition, has the time,
space, and inclination to carry along the modest
extra weight.

This is beginning to sound, I suppose, like a
diatribe against the highly popular dehydrated and
freeze-dried foods that are sold in backpacking-
supply stores. I don't mean it that way. I don't particularly like the taste of many of those foods. They
have what can only be called a "freeze-dried taste"
and odor, not to mention consistency—and I certainly don't like their prices.

But such foods are definitely useful on many occasions: on long trips when a great deal of food
must be carried along, or even short trips in winter
when much of the room in the pack must be taken

up with extra clothing. Whenever space and weight are very important, foods from backpacking-supply stores are virtually indispensable. Consider the case of Mountain House's relatively new line of freeze-dried and compressed "discs" of food: a disc of "shrimp Creole" weighs 4.2 ounces, then recombines with water in the woods to produce 20 ounces of food.

What is offered in this book is another way to make shrimp Creole, along with quite a few other dishes. You'll find yourself carrying more than 4.2 ounces per meal, but the cost will be considerably less and the taste quite different. And you might have some fun in the process.

I am not an intuitive cook. An intuitive cook can walk into a kitchen (or, for our purposes, step out-side a tent in the morning), check on what's avail-able, and nine times out of ten come up with a meal that is good-tasting and imaginative. My wife is such a cook, and although I have tried to turn myself *into* such a cook, I find that I consistently fail. So, like the majority of the cooks in the world, I fall back on trial and error, with a lot of the latter, and on tried and proven recipes and techniques.

There is nothing at all wrong with sticking with what you know will work. I had the enviable oppor-tunity several years ago to serve as, you might say, a professional cook. Indeed, it was an offer I couldn't refuse, inasmuch as it was extended by the United States Army.*

---

* If you ever wondered how the army gets its cooks, I am now able to reveal the secret. I went through a vast battery of tests at five in the morning to determine my aptitude, if any. One of the tests showed that I could type 78 words a minute with two fingers. "You're a natural for clerk-typist,

As an army cook, I suddenly found myself on the receiving end of all the insults the troops like to save for the people who cook their food, and also I was able to see why so many of those complaints were justified. If you followed the recipes, the food almost always was solid and palatable. But many institutional cooks—and not just in the army—never follow the rules. There was one fellow whom I particularly remember; his remedy for every recipe was half a bottle of Texas Pete Hot Sauce. Another one poured enough salt into everything to create a regiment of hypertensives.

The point is: By all means break the rules, but only if you know what the rules are before you break them.

Relying on what's tried and proven does not mean automatic blandness. Some of the recipes here are quite spicy; practically all of them can be made more or less spicy, according to your individual taste. Perhaps the greatest and best difference between the foods that may be prepared from these recipes and those freeze-dried delicacies that may be found in the backpacking stores is that many of these meals utilize the same inexpensive and extremely lightweight herbs and spices that are used in cooking at home. This, as much as anything else, helps to eliminate the "freeze-dried taste" from the meals and makes them taste more like something you'd get at home or in a restaurant.

The best example of this little bit of palatal deception may be found in the dishes that utilize curry

---

Private Powledge," said a grinning sergeant. "We're sending you to cook school at Fort Dix." Why, I foolishly inquired, not send me to typing school? If I could do 78 with two fingers, just think what I could do with ten, etc. "Because we need cooks this month," said the sergeant.

powder. The meat in those recipes is far from fresh—
and one dish has no meat at all—but the addition
of a relatively small amount of curry powder, which
weighs next to nothing and takes up virtually no
room, changes the entire character of the meal—for
the better, I hope you'll agree.

When you're putting together a how-to-do-it book,
as a cooking guide is bound to be, there is some
obligation to inform the reader about the relative
costs involved—costs of food, utensils, and, most
important, backpacking stoves. And yet, with the
economy behaving as it has in recent years, it seems
absurd to quote exact prices, since they almost certainly will become immediately obsolete. Where
prices are listed here, they refer to the situation in
the middle of 1977.

A few other points:

All foods, materials, stoves, and other assorted
pieces of equipment used in the compilation of this
book were paid for by the author. No manufacturers
were solicited for "sample" merchandise, and none
volunteered.

The lack of payola has left me free to criticize
equipment and foods where I felt criticism was due.
It also left me free to heap a little praise here and
there. For instance: Fully half the recipes in this
book wouldn't be here if someone hadn't invented
Cup-a-Soup for Thomas J. Lipton, Inc., a few years
ago, and particularly Cream of Mushroom Cup-a-
Soup.

Another giant debt is owed to a book that should
be owned by anyone who eats: *The Joy of Cooking*,
by Irma S. Rombauer and Marion Rombauer Becker.
Originally published by Bobbs-Merrill in 1931, this
book is a classic. Irma is no longer around, and more

recently her daughter, Marion, has assembled the latest revised edition (called, simply, *Joy of Cooking*). The new edition is available in paperback, and few people have an excuse not to have it around, as a reference work if for no other reason.

And while I'm at it, let me extend my apologies to those people who are hard-core natural-food lovers. I worry, too—perhaps not as much as I should—about the strange-sounding ingredients that go into much of the food we consume, and in the recipes that follow I have made an effort to steer clear of products that sound like your childhood chemistry set. But I probably haven't steered clear enough for a lot of people.* I suspect that one reason I have not become a full-fledged convert to the natural-food way of life is that I have never felt comfortable in a natural-food or "health-food" store. There is too much of a tendency in those places, I think, to make outlandish nutritional and health claims; too much of a tendency, as in some of our more strident religious and political groups, to look with scorn on those who are *not* full-fledged converts; and, far too much of a tendency to charge outrageous prices.

Another comment on the light weight of backpacking foods: Every effort has been made here to choose materials that are light in weight and that will not break your back when you carry them into

* The components of Lipton Cream of Mushroom Cup-a-Soup, for instance, are: "Spray dried vegetable fat (vegetable fat, corn syrup solids, sodium caseinate, mono and diglycerides, dipotassium phosphate, sodium silico aluminate, artificial flavor and color), modified starch, whey solids, nonfat milk solids, monosodium glutamate, salt, vegetable gum, natural and artificial flavors, buttermilk solids, dehydrated mushrooms, caramel color." The law requires that ingredients be listed in descending order of quantity, so that means there are more "natural and artificial flavors," whatever those are, in cream of mushroom soup than there are mushrooms.

the woods. It stands to reason, therefore, that what is left over after you finish your meal—cans, plastic bags, paper or foil pouches, and the like—will not break your back on the return trip. In other words, carry your trash out. There may have been a day when it was not a cardinal sin to bury cans in the woods, but those days have long since disappeared. Any backpacker worthy of the name has an absolute obligation to carry out every inorganic item that he or she carries into the woods. Many of us take that a step further: It's practically no trouble at all to take along an extra garbage bag and to tuck it through a pack strap on the way out of the woods so that we can pick up some of the mess that others have left behind.

Unless otherwise noted, each of the recipes makes one serving. That's because I do most of my back-packing alone, and I find it easier to make up my meals that way. It should be easy to double or triple the ingredients, or to take along a large can of tuna instead of a small one, if more people are going along.

And a final word on how the recipes were tested. Each dish was cooked a number of times on a kitchen stove while the inevitable adjustments were being made in seasonings, cooking time, amount of water, and so forth. Some did not make it past this point (generally I could easily spot the failures; they were the ones even the cat wouldn't touch).

When a final recipe was achieved, the meal was cooked again, this time under what, for me, are actual field conditions: out of doors, in my faithful cookpot, over my frequently faithful stove, usually on ground that refuses to be level and with a tricky wind trying to put the fire out. Only when the meal could be properly cooked under true backpacking conditions was it included in the book.

Instructions, by the way, are based on the time needed to cook foods at, or no more than 2,000 feet above, sea level. Since water boils at lower temperatures at higher altitudes (194°F at 10,000 feet, rather than sea level's 212°F), high-altitude cooking will require more boiling time. This should not present much of a problem with most of the recipes in this book, since practically all of the foods being boiled (rice, soups, noodles, and the like) may be tested for doneness by tasting.

One big advantage of this method of multiple tests is that conditions in the field are often very much unlike those in a nice, warm, undrafty kitchen with classical music going in the background. An enormous difference is that backpackers have to cope, by and large, with stoves that are incapable of truly simmering, whereas a modern kitchen range thinks nothing of throttling down to the barest flame. Consequently you won't find any recipes here that call for sautéeing onions by the most delicious method (in a mixture of half oil, half butter, covered in a skillet, at the lowest possible flame for an hour or so). You will find some information on how to get some dehydrated onion flakes perked up and into a stew or two without burning them to a crisp over a backpacking stove that has two positions: Towering Inferno and Off.

I hope that last image—the comparison between delicately sautéed onions and the infinitely grosser dehydrated and flaked variety—doesn't put you off and keep you from reading on. Trail dining is a compromise. You're there for the backpacking and for whatever the backpacking does for or to you, not for the gourmet dining. The food is highly secondary.

But there's no need to subsist entirely on crunchy

peanut butter and dried apricots, either. With relatively little effort and outlay of cash, you can take those food breaks on the trail—particularly the one at the end of the day, when you shuck your boots and think about all those hills you climbed and how good the sleeping bag's going to feel—with something approaching a little excitement.

2

THE SYSTEM

I realize now, as I see it up there in writing, that "The System" is a somewhat pretentious way to describe the situation. It's really quite simple and natural, hardly more complicated or "systematic" than buying food for preparation at home. Essentially it consists of this:

· Purchasing ingredients in supermarkets and/or (if you're lucky enough to live near them) at ethnic or otherwise specialized grocery stores. Your shopping is done with an eye toward light weight, palatability, and nutrition. And, of course, reasonable cost.

· Parceling out and repackaging your ingredients at home so that they may be recombined easily and without confusion or waste into meals once you're in the woods.

The trip to the supermarket, even for those of us who make it frequently and who therefore ought to have developed antibodies against it, can be a traumatic experience. But it is essential for the recipes that follow.

A modern American supermarket is a strange conglomeration of objects, shapes, feelings, messages,

temptations, and atmospheres, not all of them con-
ducive to the best mental (or physical) health. For
one thing (and this fact has not been lost on the
advertisers and packagers of America's multi-billion-
dollar food industry), the place trades heavily on
the shopper's sense of guilt and needs for fulfillment.
It fairly well forces on the shopper the opportunity
to do something good and pleasurable for the people
in her or his life—to buy food for them, to make
sure that they never leave the table hungry or
unsatisfied.

But the supermarket is also the lurking place for
countless deceptive, misleading, and fraudulent advertising claims and marketing practices: brightly
colored boxes with glorified "suggested servings"
pictured on them; 28-ounce quarts; shortweighting;
ham-watering; insect and rodent excreta; pricing and
weighting techniques so confusing that they must be
deliberately so; widespread inaction on the part of
governmental agencies at all levels that are paid to
keep the food business honest—plus, on top of all
that, interminable waits in checkout lines that raise
your anxiety level to the point where you don't even
care whether the cashier gets the prices right. You
just want to get out of there.

I live in what the social scientists and bureaucrats
like to call a "central-city" area, so many of the
supermarkets I frequent are all those things, plus
filthy. The situation appears to be somewhat better
in suburbia—in those huge, plastic supermarkets
with enormous parking lots with all the stray shopping carts standing around because people are too
lazy or, perhaps, resentful to push them back to the
store.

It apparently is the feeling of the marketers and
advertisers that the suburban American who does

the cooking—the person commonly referred to as the "housewife"—is incredibly dumb and lazy, and furthermore is so gullible that he or she will fall for any advertising message promising to make cooking less of a chore.

So it is not surprising that these suburban stores are chock full of the sort of goodies (or baddies, depending on how you look at them) that will be helpful for backpackers: packets that become soup with the mere addition of some boiling water (you don't even have to open a can, much less start your soup from scratch and simmer it into tomatoey perfection all day in a big old pot); mysterious compounds that claim to "help" tuna fish; bottles and cans of dried substances that free you from the delicious (I think) tasks of peeling and chopping onions or delightfully unleashing the considerable inner powers of garlic cloves by crushing them with the side of a Chinese cleaver.*

So, if you're a city-bound backpacker, it might be worth your while to do a little reverse commuting one day and go to a big, plastic supermarket in the suburbs. Take plenty of money, allow yourself at least half a day, and watch out for the stray shopping carts in the parking lot.

Similarly, if you're a suburbanite, it wouldn't hurt to spend a while wandering around some of the "central city's" ethnic enclaves. The neighborhood I live in, in Brooklyn, has a large Italian population, many of its members first-generation. Although I'm

* As an indication of how far this has got out of hand: I found myself not long ago at the home of a friend and relative, and I offered to cook a shrimp gumbo. I started making a list, from memory, of the ingredients I would need, and as I did so I asked my hostess if she had each of the items. When I got to garlic—which at home I always use in its bulb form—my hostess said, "No, I don't think I have a bottle of that."

not Italian, I automatically benefit in several ways from my neighbors' refusal to settle for food, spices, and condiments that are bland, tasteless, and plastic. Not only can I buy for our regular, at-home meals fresh eggplant and broccoli (and garlic that somehow magically avoided getting put into a bottle) every day of the year; I also have a large choice of pastas that are helpful in the backpacker's kitchen, along with cans of delicious beef and little tins of basil and cheese that I have never seen in a supermarket.

And when I backpack across the Brooklyn Bridge into lower Manhattan, and into the narrow, excited streets of Chinatown, there's even more: dried shrimp, which weigh practically nothing (and which I dislike, but others love); oriental noodles, which quickly combine with boiling water; and (to my mind best of all) dried Chinese mushrooms, which are so light in weight that you practically have to tie them down to something, but which, when rehydrated, offer meals a genuine mushroomy taste that simply cannot be achieved with anything else.

Even closer to my home, on a locally famous Brooklyn thoroughfare named Atlantic Avenue, is an authentic Middle Eastern neighborhood, with stores that serve the Middle Eastern populations of the New York metropolitan area. There I can buy the delicious grain product known as couscous, and cashews that taste like cashews, not like something that came out of a can (I have my choice of those that are unroasted and unsalted, unroasted and salted, roasted and salted, and roasted and unsalted; the cost is half that of dime-store cashews); and a dozen different curries, along with enough various sorts of flour, priced very reasonably, to make a "health-food" store wince.

A twenty-minute subway ride will take me to

Yorkville, the German-American neighborhood in Manhattan, and I can sample some of the delicacies there. Knorr, a European outfit, makes especially good dried soups, and their potato-pancake mix is delicious.*

So part of "The System" is no system at all but simply an inclination toward following your nose, your instinct, and your imagination into places that sell food, wandering up and down the aisles and letting your eyes skim along the shelves, looking at all those boxes, bags, and cans with a new thought in mind: Is there any way I can use this in backpacking? You may be surprised at what develops. And your taste buds might be quite pleasantly surprised at what turns up in your cooking pot.

The range of what you will find that will be useful is likely to be somewhat limited. Many of the main dishes I have developed here are variations on a few central themes, the themes consisting of a starch (quick-cooking rice, spaghetti, macaroni, noodles, instant mashed potatoes), some source of protein, usually one that comes in a can (tuna, chicken, turkey, fish or shellfish, Vienna sausage, but also peanuts, cashews, soy nuts, and the like), with the starch and the protein being bound together and made more palatable, not to mention a lot less dry, by a base of sauce, soup, or gravy. Plus herbs, spices, and what dried vegetables as may be available to give the dish a little character and to make up for the unavoidable blandness.

In other words, your pretty basic one-pot, stewlike meal, which, if you approach it with a little imagination, won't be a drab and tasteless affair at

---

* There is a section of recipes, later on, called "Exotica," which deals with some of these products.

all but a pleasant and maybe even memorable way to end a physically tiring and emotionally uplifting day in the woods.

For those who have access to specialized backpacking stores, and to larger quantities of money than does the typical frugal backpacker, some slight enlargement of these horizons may be managed. By this I mean the use, in addition to the supermarket provisions, of a few items from your favorite outfitter. These would include precooked and compressed bars of meat and bacon, and packets and cans of freeze-dried chicken, ham, meat patties, meatballs, and the like.

And freeze-dried peas. I have tried a variety of freeze-dried and dehydrated backpacking foods in my time, and I have found most of them to be not worth the trouble. Freeze-dried sweet corn is the worst I have ever encountered. I inflicted some of this on myself and my daughter while on a short camping excursion not long ago, and I doubt that she will ever forgive me. I *know I* never will.

People who love corn on the cob, and who have access to the truly fresh variety, have a saying about how to cook it: First you start the water boiling. *Then* you pick the corn. There's a lot of truth in that exaggeration. Corn starts to turn into cardboard the moment it's torn from its stalk. So you can imagine what happens when it is picked, shipped, freeze-dried, sealed in a plastic bag, shipped some more, and placed on a shelf in a backpacking emporium for a few weeks. The final product is a sugary mess with the texture and consistency of the plastic that is used to pack cameras and transistor radios.

Freeze-dried peas are different. They come across, without a doubt, as freeze-dried, as opposed to the fresh variety, or even the frozen or canned sort. But they still manage to say "I am a pea" when you bite into one of them, which ought to be enough for your typical backpacker. For that reason, I have included freeze-dried peas in several recipes.* They may be considered optional ingredients; in none of the recipes is their presence mandatory.

Once the menu is set for a backpacking trip, and once the ingredients are assembled, it's a virtual certainty that everything must be repackaged for the trail.

Why? Because unless you are fortunate enough to have the use of a pack animal, or unless you are one of those people who sport about in a plastic motor home, calling yourself a "camper" but never setting your feet on the dangerous and dirty old ground, it would be absurd for you to go into the woods carrying your food in the containers in which you bought it.

When people go into a supermarket in this country, most of the time they are not buying food at all. They are purchasing images they saw advertised on television or somewhere else; they are purchasing status (beef stroganoff sounds high-class to people who were brought up on beef stew); they are buying a pretty picture (a "serving suggestion") they see on a can or a box. Most of all, they are buying water and air.

---

* The peas I have used, and would recommend, are packed by Rich-Moor Corporation. A 2-ounce package (which sold for 80 cents in 1976—that's $6.40 a pound if you want to make yourself depressed) contains, in addition to the peas, some sugar, salt, and sodium bisulfate. In their freeze-dried condition the peas are about the size of regular peas, but because most of their water has been removed they are considerably lighter in weight.

Water is important for the processing and packing of many foods, of course, although it's always rather shocking to read the ingredient list on a can of, say, "beef stew" and see that you're buying more water than anything else. Air is another matter. Despite the claims of some marketing genius that the contents of a box of cereal or rice or pasta may "settle during shipment," it is obvious that many food manufacturers and packers are trying to deceive consumers with the sizes of their packages. Sometimes I have found as much as a third of the volume of a package given over to "contents settling."

The traveler of trails can't afford to carry all this excess packaging around. It therefore becomes necessary to repackage, in smaller and more efficient bundles, most of the constituent parts of trail meals.* Directions for doing this are in the following chapter.

"The System," in addition to relying heavily on supermarket foods and repackaging, is based, too, on another practice that most backpackers will not find foreign. Emphasis is being placed here, as it is elsewhere in the literature of backpacking, on the one big meal that woods travelers seem to most look forward to—usually the meal that is eaten at the end of the day.

Maybe you're different, but for me and for others I've met and consulted with in the woods, breakfast and lunch are considered little more than nec-

* There are several exceptions to this, and they will be pointed out at appropriate points in the recipes. Dried soup mixes, for instance, usually come from the store in cardboard boxes that contain several foil pouches of mix. It's easy to throw away the outer box, but you want to leave the mix inside the pouches. They take up very little room and keep the dehydrated contents from picking up moisture until you're ready to use them.

essary fueling stops. They are meals that no one, even the most dedicated breakfast-skipper, wants to miss in the woods, because they so obviously produce the calories and other nutrients that give us energy to continue down the trail or the river.

But neither have I ever met anyone who wanted to make a big deal out of either meal. One excellent reason is the matter of cleaning up. If you're walking a trail for, say, three days, camping in a different spot each night, you want to get going in the morning as soon as you've eaten and pushed the sleeping bag down inside its stuff sack. You don't want to spend a lot of time cleaning pots and pans. It's the same situation at lunch, only more so.

The obvious exception to all of this is when you decide to take a day off from walking and stay in one place. Then breakfast becomes a great feast, or perhaps a gourmet orgy if you're handy at catching trout.

But basically it's the evening meal that counts. This is the one that comes at the end of the walking day, the one you eat when you feel that you deserve a break tonight—a meal to take a little time over, to relish a while, to anticipate, to explore for subtle tastes; a meal you eat with your feet tucked into the sleeping bag against the evening chill, while you consider the things you saw and did that day and contemplate the things you'll see and do tomorrow.

3

THE COOK'S TOOLS

The tools of backpacking are both a delight and a pain in the neck.

They're delightful because the proper equipment makes backpacking safer, less tiring, and more fun. They're a pain in the neck—or, more accurately, in the back—because the more equipment you strap onto that back, presumably in an effort to increase your enjoyment of the woods, the harder backpacking becomes. So you quickly arrive at the point where you realize that lightness, more in backpacking than in practically any other sport, is absolutely crucial.

And so you spend a good deal of time poring over the catalogues of the big mail-order backpacking suppliers, comparing weights and volumes and specifications, determining in your mind whether this 4-ounce "survival" knife is really all that necessary to your survival, whether you really want to carry along that delightful little monocular, even though it does weigh far less than half a pound.

There are, of course, forces at work to tempt you away from making any such rational distinctions and decisions. There are persons at large among backpackers, just as there are those rampant in all other sports, who would make equipment more important than the use to which it is put—more important than the mountain you work so hard to climb, more important than the clear, pure spring where you quench your thirst, more important than the sunset you so richly deserve at the end of the day.

These are the people who ruined downhill skiing by making it a fashion-conscious event rather than an exhilarating way to coast silently down the side of a mountain. These are the people who would consider it not only unfashionable but close to un-American to jog to the corner for the newspaper in anything but name-brand sneakers and a uniform with a stripe down the side. These are the people who tell you it's wrong—actually *wrong*—to go cross-country skiing in blue jeans. Only knickers will do.

These people, and the half-snobbish, half-insecure attitude they articulate, have not yet made significant inroads into backpacking, although they're giving it a good try. Perhaps it's because backpackers—true backpackers, not folks who amble around the singles bars in "survival clothes"—have small or nonexistent audiences in front of whom to show off. If you're really in the woods, very few people are going to notice that your gaiters are actually old army-surplus puttees, or that your junk is all riding inside a $20 rucksack from J. C. Penney instead of Kelty's most expensive creation.

It's the same with the basic tools of the backpacker's kitchen: More does not necessarily mean better. Very often, in fact, it means worse.

Please bear all that in mind as you wander through the following list of tools for the backpacker's kitchen. My list does not have to be your list; it's just the one that has evolved for me in the past several years. It works for me. It is subject to constant changes as new, and sometimes even improved, equipment comes on the market.

Before we discuss the list, we have to consider briefly a crucially important part of backpacking and of backpacking cookery: The New Backpacking Ethic.

When I was a boy in the Forties, living on the edge of a smallish-sized city in the South, where "the woods" started just a few hundred yards away, there were no magazines for backpackers. All our equipment came from army-navy stores. No one, to my knowledge, even used the term "backpacking"; the word was "camping," and it was understood that the experience you sought had to do with living in one spot in a tent in the woods, not with getting to that spot under your own steam. *That* was "hiking."

Colin Fletcher had not yet written his walking person's Bible. For me and for a lot of my contemporaries, the only available Scripture was a copy of the *Handbook for Boys*, the official publication of the Boy Scouts of America. On the subject of cooking your food in the woods, the handbook was quite firm: You built a fire. There were little pictures of all sorts of fires and fireplaces, from the pot-hanging-on-a-branch-suspended-between-two-forked-sticks to the old favorite, burying-potatoes-in-the-ashes-to-bake-them.

It was *assumed* that you would be building a fire when you went into the woods, just as it was *assumed* that if you wanted a comfortable night's sleep you'd cut some evergreen boughs for your mattress.

Those days, as not enough people know, are gone forever. What we have to replace them is something loosely known as The New Backpacking Ethic. It's easy to remember—not at all complicated. The cur-

rent editions of the Boy Scout handbook are full of
it. The new ethic simply states that when we go into
the woods, we have to respect the fragility of those
woods. Thirty years ago, even twenty years ago, we
had some excuses. We didn't know how fragile the
woods were. But then came the publication of Rachel
Carson's *Silent Spring* in *The New Yorker*, and in
book form in 1962, and everything changed dras-
tically.

So we don't cut bough beds any more. Nor do
we bury our garbage in the woods. And neither, on
most occasions, do we build fires—either the roar-
ing, sitting-around-talking-into-the-night variety or
the simple cooking type.

There are some places where fire-making is obviously all right. Beaches with good supplies of drift-
wood may be among them, as are public campsites
with formal fireplaces and supplies of cut firewood
or plenty of winterkill. But most places in the back
country, including more or less formal campsites
along maintained trails, should not be subjected to
open fires for the simple reason that there are too
few trees and too many of *us*.

Campfires may have been possible back when I
was a boy, reading my Boy Scout handbook, but
now there are millions of us, and the millions are
multiplying, constantly growing, using the woods
each year, and the woods we are using are constantly shrinking in size. It might have been possible,
a generation ago, to ignore a solitary blackened spot
beside a trail. But now, the scars left by a dozen
blazes constructed in fire rings (the circles of rocks
that campers gather to contain their fires) last for
years, and can permanently disfigure a beautiful
mountain meadow. It's interesting to note that trail
clubs, when they conduct periodic cleanup hikes, now

keep records not only of how many bags of garbage and trash they have collected, but also of how many fire rings they have dismantled.*

So, if you have an appreciation for the new back-packing ethic and a respect for the woods, nine times out of ten you will find the small backpacker's stove to be at the center of your traveling kitchen.

THE STOVE

What you look for in a backpacker's stove is de-pendability, light weight, efficiency, and ease of op-

---

* All this talk of the new ethic seems rather obvious, and I feel a little foolish even bringing it up. But there are a lot of people who apparently haven't received the message. Even more tragically, there are some people who continue to preach the *old*, destructive message, despite abundant evidence that to do so is to invite the ruination of the wilderness. A year ago I encountered a clutch of Boy Scouts on a trail in New York State. Their leader, a grown man in the big version of the Scout uniform, was showing the kids how to attack and eventually chop down a green sapling with an ax that was big enough to build a log cabin. Even worse, there is loose on the public a paperback book called *Home in Your Pack*, by Bradford Angier, which is every bit as potentially destructive as my old Scout handbook. Angier's book was copyrighted in 1965, which means it was written at a time when there may have been some feeble justification for not knowing about the new backpacking ethic. But the paperback version came out in 1972, and has gone through several printings since then, which means there is no excuse for Angier's dangerous advice. Furthermore, the book's sub-title is "The Modern Handbook of Backpacking." Among Angier's modern tips: An "experienced woodsman" builds a bough bed of evergreens; the hiker is frequently advised to "locate" poles for this or that reason; tent pegs may be cut "where there is forest growth"; and, the campfire is all-important. For Angier, thoughts of the fire are "what remain most fondly in our mind after a wilderness hike." He at least acknowledges the existence of the backpacking stove: It "is often the answer for campers who hike beyond the tree line." Angier should be sentenced to dismantle fire rings for ten years for statements like those.

eration. Unfortunately, it is almost impossible to make those determinations at first hand without shelling out an awful lot of money for backpacking stoves. The little devils cost around $30 each at the moment,* so owning even one of them can be quite a strain.

There are, however, some sources of comparative information on stoves, so a person getting into the sport can walk into the store with his or her eyes a little less than wide open. Those sources include:

· Colin Fletcher's beautiful book, *The New Complete Walker* (Knopf, 1974). It contains 111 pages of information on the backpacker's kitchen, much of it about specific stoves and other kitchen implements.

· Harvey Manning's *Backpacking: One Step at a Time* (Vintage, 1973).

Less detailed but still helpful comparisons and specifications are offered in the catalogues of at least two of the large mail-order houses: Eastern Mountain Sports, Inc. (1047 Commonwealth Avenue, Boston, Massachusetts, 02215), and Recreational Equipment, Inc. (1525 Eleventh Avenue, Seattle, Washington, 98122). These catalogues offer the additional benefit of quoting current prices in a market where costs seem to be spiraling eternally upward.

The absolutely best comparative information, as of this writing, is contained in *Backpacker* magazine, issues 15 and 16 (June and August, 1976). *Backpacker*'s editors conducted detailed tests on thirty-four stoves, and they present every imaginable scrap of information on them, along with some tips on how to keep from killing yourself with a stove. Any

* That's as of 1977. The same stoves, three years before, tended to cost approximately half as much. But then the industry discovered that backpacking was popular, and you know what happened after that.

serious backpacker should have access to these tests. For that matter, any serious backpacker should subscribe to *Backpacker* (65 Adams Street, Bedford Hills, New York, 10507).

Then there are my own, somewhat limited comparisons—limited mainly by the cost of the devices. My own trials of a number of stoves in the field have been enough to convince me of a few things, though. One of them is that manufacturers' claims as to a stove's capacity and efficiency are often at variance with reality.

Another is that several of the stoves seem to have been designed by people who never have used them and who don't have the slightest idea of what backpacking is about.

Another is that stoves which use "gasoline" (or, more correctly, white gasoline or Coleman-type fuel) are superior in almost all applications to stoves that operate on pressurized gases (usually butane).

And another is that, among the gasoline stoves, the Optimus was for years my favorite brand, and that among the several stoves produced by Optimus, the Model 99 is the one I trust most. More than trust: practically cherish.* (I will explain later why I say the Optimus *was* my favorite.)

Perhaps the most important of those findings is the alleged superiority of Coleman-fuel-type stoves to those that run on pressure cans of butane. (I'm not even mentioning propane here. Propane is stored under great pressure, requiring that it be bottled in containers that are too heavy for backpackers to

* This I suppose, is where the battle lines will be drawn. I can almost hear the multitudinous lovers of Svea 123s muttering now, plotting against me, planning my ultimate humiliation. I haven't even *mentioned* their little darling stove! I can only say, at this point, that the battle has just begun. You'll see why later in this book.

consider. It's a great favorite, however, among those who take off in trailers and motor homes and consider themselves "campers.")

For many people, butane is considerably easier to operate. You screw in a gas cartridge, or tighten a collar that connects the burner mechanism to the cartridge; you strike a match, open a valve, and you immediately have a flame. The flame is ready for cooking, and it can usually be controlled from a simmer to a blast with a simple turn of the valve. When you use up the gas in a cartridge, you unscrew it and plug in another. If you turn the stove off and then need to relight it to heat up some water or leftovers, you simply light another match.

With a gasoline stove, it's quite a different proposition. You fill a tank with Coleman-type fuel. With most lightweight stoves, you must then extract an eyedropperful of fuel (or obtain it in some other way; there are dozens of them) and squirt it into a little brass cup at the base of the burner. You light the fuel in the cup (making sure that you have first screwed the cap back on the main tank). It flares up, creating something of a blaze but, more important, creating heat that builds up pressure in the tank. Only when proper pressure has been created—after one to three minutes, ordinarily—are you able to get down to real business and open the fuel valve.

Then, if everything has been done correctly up until this point, vaporized and pressurized fuel will spew from a tiny hole, will ignite there, and will create a powerful flame to cook your freeze-dried surf-'n'-turf or whatever you brought along. It takes more time, more motions, and more memory than the butane method. And if you want to relight the stove soon after shutting it down, you usually have to wait a while for the generator to cool off.

If your gasoline stove breaks down, there is a whole series of parts, resembling the carburetor on a Volkswagen Beetle, that may or may not be at fault, and that may or may not be fixable in the woods. A butane stove consists largely of just a valve to let the butane out of the cartridge and to mix it with the surrounding air.

Obviously, the butane stove is better, right?

Not necessarily. There are quite a few drawbacks —enough of them, in my mind, to severely restrict my own use of such stoves. I take one along only on casual hikes when I know I'll want to heat up some water for soup at lunchtime or when I think I'll want to stop and make some tea.

Butane loses efficiency as temperatures approach freezing, which means it is less useful in cooler weather—and remember that in the woods, cooler weather can come even in the summertime. The empty cartridges are a pain to pack out, and they *must* be packed out.

Worst of all, the heat output of butane stoves (and, thus, their ability to boil water within anything like a decent period of time) declines as pressure within the cartridge drops, meaning that you won't get the same action out of a half-empty cartridge as you get out of a full one. And since, on some stoves, you cannot remove a cartridge until it's empty, you may find yourself some icy morning waiting interminably for water to boil for that life-giving cup of coffee or tea. It can be quite a painful wait.

But what's painful for me might be not painful for you. Maybe the ease of operation is worth it. Maybe the differences in boiling times are not significant enough to make you undertake the patient and sometimes frustrating care of a gasoline stove. Here, for the record, are the general descriptions and boiling times for some of the stoves with which I have become familiar:

The first of two butane stoves is the Primus Ranger 2255, an ungainly-looking fellow that somewhat resembles a praying mantis. In traveling shape, it forms something of a cylinder about 13 inches long and 4 inches in diameter. When you get where you're going, you fold out two tubular legs to form a tripod; in the third leg you screw a butane cartridge; and at the top of all this is the burning stage. The Primus weighs 15¼ ounces without a fuel canister. I have found canisters that fit the stove in a couple of sizes: 9½ ounces, which contains 6½ ounces of fuel, and slightly over 11 ounces, which contains 8 ounces of fuel. Cartridges may be unscrewed from the stove before they are completely empty.

The Ranger costs somewhere around $10 to $15, which makes it attractive to the hard-pressed backpacker. I suspect that one reason for its relatively low cost is its looks. It looks foolish, and I cannot imagine why anyone would want to buy it. But I have found it to be a cornucopia of British Thermal Units; if I were not prejudiced against butane stoves, I would use this one.

I hooked up the Ranger with a fresh 9½-ounce cartridge of fuel and conducted eight "burns," of 10, 15, and 20 minutes each, which were designed to simulate use of the stove for typical backpacking meals. The cartridge burned for 114 minutes and then expired, suddenly and without warning. During each of the tests, I set on the burning stage a small Sigg aluminum pot (we'll talk about that later) containing 16 ounces of water at room temperature. The pot was not covered. (That was so I could be sure to tell when boiling had actually started. Ordinarily you'd want to cover the pot, in which case it would take less time to achieve a boil.)

The first time the Ranger was fired up, it brought the water to a boil* in 3 minutes and 10 seconds, which is pretty good by anybody's standards. The second time, although pressure in the cartridge was lower, it took only 3 minutes. This proves another point that should be made here, which is that quite often unnatural phenomena occur in conjunction with backpacking stoves. But by the eighth and final burn, the Ranger was taking 5 minutes and 5 seconds to boil the water.

The second butane stove with which I have some experience is the Globe Trotter, manufactured by Camping Gaz International. This one is distributed by Wonder Corporation of America, which is situated in Stamford, Connecticut. Wonder is one of several U.S.-based firms that import and distribute backpacking equipment from abroad. In their specific case, the emphasis is on gas-powered stoves and lanterns. A complaint, not at all limited to the Wonder people, is that their responsibility seems limited to selling you the item and little more.

The Globe Trotter is made in France, and if you buy one and are dissatisfied with it, you may want to write to Information du Consommateur, on rue Chateaubriand, 75008, Paris. Or you can phone them at 359.72–02. All of which is a reminder that with most backpacking stoves—and all of them that I have owned that are imported—there is no such thing as a warranty or a guarantee.

---

* By "boil," I mean a full, vigorous, rolling boil, with big bubbles roiling the surface of the water. This test, and all the others unless noted otherwise, was conducted at about 30 feet above sea level on a warmish day (60 to 80°F), with not enough of a breeze to make much difference.

The Globe Trotter weighs 16½ ounces and has a height and a diameter of about 4 inches each. Its cartridges, which fit only the Gaz appliances, are small blue cans weighing 5½ ounces and containing 3⅛ ounces of fuel. A problem is that the cartridges are held on by a clamping mechanism and may not be removed from the burner assembly until they are empty. An even bigger problem, in my estimation, is that the cartridges are by no means easy to find, in this country, at least. Since I obtained my Globe Trotter, in 1976, I have checked backpacking-supply stores, sporting-goods places, and discount stores in the eastern part of the country to see if they carry the GT cartridge, as it is called. Very few did. A backpacker planning excursions to other parts of the nation, then, might have difficulty obtaining fuel in a container that will fit the Globe Trotter.

What really bothered me about the stove was something I can't at all blame on the manufacturer: It's the promotion it got from the catalogue of a backpacking store I have always considered reliable. This store, in what I hope will not become the usual procedure for such ordinarily dependable outlets, called the little stove "revolutionary" and gave its weight, including fuel, as 12 ounces. If that had been true, it would truly have been revolutionary; high on the list of a backpacker's fantasies, right up there with a comfortable tent that keeps you dry and the mosquitoes away and weighs 2 ounces, is the truly lightweight stove. Unfortunately, the 12-ounce claim was about 50 percent shy of reality. The store sold the Globe Trotter for $25.

The only reason I tested the Globe Trotter at all was that I happened across one in a discount store in upstate New York one day. It was selling for $10.99, and I bought it, I suppose because I had been conditioned to believe it was worth $25, and so I thought I was getting a bargain.*

I did several burns with the Globe Trotter, as I had done with the Ranger, and I found that the butane cartridge expired after about 73 minutes, a fairly respectable time, considering its small size. But during that period, the time required to bring 16 ounces of water to a boil grew from 4 minutes, 50 seconds (with a full cartridge), to 6 minutes, 50 seconds (on the last burn). Toward the end, the vigorous boil disappeared entirely, and then, a few minutes later, it returned, then faded forever.

If I had been cooking a real dinner out in the woods just then, I would have been somewhat frustrated, since for several minutes there was not enough heat to really cook on, but I couldn't hook up a new cartridge until the old one had gone through its entire death scene.

---

* This is not an inducement for shopping for backpacking equipment at discount stores. Often the merchandise, backpacking and otherwise, that is found in such places is of low quality, not to mention battered and beaten and picked apart, dropped, cracked, broken, and split. One exception is Coleman fuel; I would buy it nowhere else, because the prices are almost always lower. But in order to buy the Globe Trotter stove from a discount joint in upstate New York, I had to find one that was complete—no easy task, since countless other shoppers had picked away at the stock, and the clerks had made no effort to see that everything was together. I found a box that was open—that wasn't difficult—and extracted the instruction sheet. It was one of those multi-language documents composed by a person who was studying to become a turnip, but from the pictures I was able to determine what parts were supposed to be there. From surrounding boxes I was able to piece together a complete Globe Trotter. Of course, if I had bought the machine from my always-condsidered-reliable backpacking store, they would have sold me a complete stove in the first place, or, if something had been missing, would have given me a substitute—all for the $14 extra I would have paid.

The Globe Trotter comes with a couple of small, lightweight aluminum pots, which form the top and bottom of the stove when it is packed for traveling, and which hold about 21 ounces of fluid each. There is a wire pot handle. When the whole thing is put together, a strap is supposed to be placed around it to keep it from falling apart. But the fellow who designed the pots was the cousin of the fellow who wrote the instructions, and he neglected to attach enough strap guides to the pots. So you put it all together, cinch the strap tight, and then watch as the entire device collapses into its component parts. It's incredible that the office of the Consommateur let this one off the drawing boards, but that's the French Free Enterprise System, I guess.

There are, of course, many more butane stoves on the market—*Backpacker* magazine tested eleven of them in its comprehensive roundup, and it is certain that the booming market will bring even more into the stores and catalogues—but the Ranger and the Globe Trotter are probably fairly typical. Both machines are extremely simple to operate, and that's certainly typical of butane stoves. The problems they present, not the least of which is the uncertain availability of their fuel, are also, unfortunately, typical. But it's a compelling argument that the butane stoves are terribly easy to light, in temperate weather, at least,* and you may be delighted with yours.

* Butane has the unfortunate property of refusing to vaporize at temperatures below 32°F, which makes it difficult to use in colder weather. One approach to this problem is to figure out some way to keep the fuel warm, and the Alp stove has taken this approach. I have not used an Alp, but Moor & Mountain, a Massachusetts mail-order supplier, says the stove employs a loop in its fuel line that preheats the gas before it reaches the burner. Proper vaporization of the fuel is then

I am much more delighted, as by now you may have noticed, with stoves that operate on Coleman-type fuel. Here, then, are some comments on a few of what are normally referred to as "gasoline," or "white gas," stoves.

The Optimus 8R was my first backpacking stove. Now its blue paint job is almost gone, and the hinge lets out a terrible squeak when I open it, but it lights with ease and cooks food along with any of the rest of them.

The 8R is from Sweden. It is, essentially, a metal box, about 5 inches by 5 by $3\frac{1}{4}$, which hinges open into a top and a bottom. In the bottom is the burner: a brass gizmo that is connected to a cylindrical fuel tank. There's a flap on the side of the box so that the tank and burner slide out and into their proper positions. Above all this are a couple of pot supports. A long-stemmed valve controls the flame and raises and lowers a tiny needle that cleans the burner head. The top part of the box serves somewhat, but not an awfully lot, as a windscreen.

The stove weighs 25 ounces with an empty fuel tank and $28\frac{1}{2}$ ounces with a full one. In 1977 the 8R cost around $28.

The procedure for lighting and operating the stove is as described before, and is similar to that for almost all such nonpump stoves. (I.e., the pressure for vaporizing the fuel and creating an intense heat comes, at first, from priming the stove with fuel or priming paste; then, when the machine has heated up sufficiently, it becomes self-pressurizing. There

---

presumably assured, even in cold weather. The stove sold for around $15. *Backpacker* magazine, in its tests, downrated the Alp considerably, calling it "serviceable" for three-season use and of "doubtful" value in the winter, and charging that the stove was "poorly made."

will be a discussion of a pump-operated stove, which obtains its initial pressure from another source, a little later.) It's helpful to carry a small eyedropper along with the 8R so that you can prime it by extracting a little fuel from the tank and depositing it in the priming cup.

Then you make absolutely sure you have secured the top on the fuel tank (if you haven't, you may be buying a new sleeping bag, tent, and eyebrows), and you touch a lighted match to the priming cup. There's a moderately blinding flash of light, and the stove is on its way to being pressurized. In half a minute or so, or at about the time the priming fuel is burned away, you open the fuel valve and, if everything's gone well, you have a good, hot, blue-green flame for cooking.

The 8R boils water in something longer than record time, but it's rather reliable. In a boiling test, conducted under the usual rules, the machine produced three separate boils in 8 minutes, 55 seconds; 6 minutes, 10 seconds; and 6 minutes, 50 seconds.

If the variation in boiling times surprises you, welcome to backpacking cookery. Perhaps the most fundamental characteristic of wilderness stoves is that they rarely do the same thing twice in the same amount of time, even under moderately controlled circumstances.

It's even difficult or impossible to determine such matters as the capacity of a fuel tank. When I first experimented with the Optimus, I led myself to believe that the capacity of its tank was 90 milliliters (about 3 ounces). But then I discovered, on subsequent fillings, that I was putting 100, 120, and finally 130 milliliters of fuel into it.

This affected the total burning time, of course. At first I was getting about 56 minutes of use out of a tankful of fuel, with the valve set at wide open. Later

it went up to almost 78 minutes. (To further compli-
cate matters, it wasn't until I had been using this
stove for a few years that I learned that you shouldn't
completely fill a tank, but should leave some room
for the air pressure you'll be building.)

So the moral is: There's nothing necessarily wrong
if there are considerable variations in burning time,
boiling time, and tank capacity.

I said I had the fuel valve set "wide open." There
is almost no other setting on the Optimus and on
many other gasoline stoves. What we call simmering
on the kitchen stove at home is virtually impossible.

The Optimus 99 is a very close cousin of the 8R.
For a long time it has been my favorite among the
small stoves. It's the same size as the 8R, and the
burner and fuel-tank mechanism are practically identical, but the 99 rests inside an aluminum box that
is lighter and handier than the original. There are no
hinges this time, and the top of the box lifts off to
become a square cooking pot (but one with rounded
corners, so you can easily clean it) that holds about
24 ounces of fluid. Included with the stove is a right-
angled piece of aluminum that serves as a windscreen. There is a small but efficient potgrabber; that
and the eyedropper you'll want to add fit inside the
box, and a strap goes around the whole thing. The
stove weighs 24½ ounces empty and 26½ ounces
with a full tank.

The business end of the 99 is, as explained before,
almost identical to the 8R. Boiling times, in my tests
and in others', are not the same, however. This is
almost certainly because of the slight differences in
the construction of the boxes that enclose the stoves.
My tests showed the 99 boiled water in 8 minutes, 12
seconds; in 11 minutes, 15 seconds; and in 8 minutes, 28 seconds.

There's one piece of forest wisdom that seems to

be passed along with some fidelity by 99 freaks, and that is this: If you plan to use the stove on the snow, or on frozen or very cold ground, efficiency is greatly enhanced if you can insulate the stove from the coldness beneath it. This is easily accomplished by cutting a small square of closed-cell foam* and carrying it along. It weighs practically nothing. The piece I use is about three times the size of the stove. This means I have room beside the stove—room that is especially welcome in wet weather—to put down my cup, my tea bag, my eating utensil, and similar items. And it *still* weighs practically nothing.

But what's the big deal? Why has the Optimus 99 been such a favorite of mine? It's certainly not what you'd call spectacular at boiling water, its fuel capacity is not astounding, and it's impossible to turn its flame down to a real simmer. I do not *know* what's the big deal. After all these years with the little machine, I cannot answer.† All I know is that I trust it more than I trust most pieces of machinery.

And then, late in the game, came the entry from Coleman. The Kansas manufacturer, whose forest-green stoves, lanterns, and iceboxes have played such prominent roles in the car, trailer, and tent-trailer "camping" market, finally came out with a stove that, it claimed, was for backpackers. It is called the Peak 1, or Model 576.

* Available from backpacking stores, where it is usually sold, in thicknesses ranging from ¼ to ½ inch, as a mattress-type pad to go under sleeping bags.

† Not only have I used the 99 for backpacking; I also used it at least twice a day while I was living in a tent and traveling with a circus around the eastern part of the United States. The 99 performed beautifully, and I was quite interested to note that the professional circus people, whose lives so fascinated me in their every detail, were themselves quite fascinated by the workings of such a little, but obscenely hot, stove.

I was skeptical at first. There's a certain snobbery, based to a great extent on actual fact, that says that no big American manufacturer could possibly develop a piece of equipment that would be useful to a *backpacker*; that only something from Sweden or Germany could do. Nevertheless, I bought one of the first Peaks to arrive on the market in the New York area. (It was made, by the way, in Canada.) I tested it. It's a first-rate stove, and it has replaced the Optimus 99 in my affections.

It is heavier than most backpacking stoves, but it has a relatively enormous fuel tank, which means you don't have to carry so much extra fuel in another container. It uses a pump to attain (and, when necessary, to maintain) pressure so that, ordinarily, no priming is needed. It is much quieter than most gasoline stoves. It has a simple windscreen that really works, even in a stiff wind. The stove puts out a tremendous amount of heat.

And you can adjust the flame down not only to a simmer but even *below* a simmer. There is a one-year limited warranty, and there are shops all over the country that can fix it and presumably carry spare parts. (There are, in the vicinity of my city, several backpacking stores that advertise that they have spare parts for Optimus and Svea stoves, but I have not found one yet that backed up the claim with anything like a comprehensive array of parts.)

Advertising copy for the Peak 1 first appeared early in 1977, and it referred to the device as "a souped-up, scaled-down backpack stove from Coleman." The cost was $27.50, which was, unfortunately, about par for backpacking stoves in 1977. It's possible, though, that lower prices might eventually be found in those large, garish, suburban discount stores once the new stove shows up in them.

The Peak 1 weighs 32 ounces empty and 39½ ounces with a full fuel tank. It's also bulkier than most other backpacking stoves; it stands about 6½ inches high and is 5 inches in diameter. It looks, in fact, like a smaller version of a fine old Coleman stove that I bought many years ago, before the back-packing revolution started in this country. It was and still is called the Coleman Sportster, and it is perfect for car and canoe camping. I keep it, and a heat drum that comes as an accessory, in the trunk of the car, ready to use if I get stuck in a snowdrift. I often found myself wishing that the Sportster were smaller and lighter so that it could be used for more light-weight camping. Now the arrival of the Peak 1 has satisfied that wish.

The big difference between the Peak 1 and many other backpacking stoves (and between it and both of the gasoline stoves described here so far) is its use of a pump to provide internal pressure. Cole-man, in a clear and easy-to-read booklet that comes with the stove, explains that some priming may be needed in subfreezing temperatures.

The Peak 1 does not come with any sort of a pot or cup that inverts over the burner head for travel-ing, and since there are several knobs and projec-tions on it, you will want to get a small stuff sack to pack the stove away in. There are no loose parts, such as eyedroppers or fuel-valve keys, on the Cole-man.

Because of the efficient fuel-regulator valve, it really is possible to cut the Peak 1 down to a low flame. Coleman claims, in its advertising, that this can allow the stove to burn for 3½ hours on a tank of fuel, which is far more than most other stoves. I tried it, with the valve at its lowest setting, which is a hair below simmer, and the stove burned for 5 hours and 10 minutes!

When I burned the stove wide open, the 10 liquid ounces of fuel lasted for around 90 minutes. But I noticed that with the Coleman, unlike the others, it's quite possible to get a lot of heat without opening the fuel valve all the way. The burner head of the Peak 1 is larger than most, which means the flame is spread over a larger area. With my small Sigg pot, in which I do most of my cooking, a flame of smaller diameter did an excellent job of covering the bottom of the pot.

Coleman claims a heat output of approximately 8500 BTU, which is meaningless to me, since none of the other stoves I have tested employ similar ratings. But my own boiling tests showed the stove to be at the top of the class. With the flame wide open, boiling times were 2 minutes, 45 seconds; 3 minutes even; and 2 minutes, 40 seconds. With the valve closed down a little, and the flame concentrated on just the bottom of the pot, it took 3 minutes, 45 seconds—still fantastic, as backpacking stoves go.

All this, in my estimation, adds up to the fact that the Coleman Peak 1 should be considered strongly by anybody who's looking for a backpacking stove. But one other characteristic, I think, pretty well clinches the argument. That's the built-in windscreen.

When you buy a backpacking stove, you take it home and try it out. A back porch, if you have one, is a great place for this. The problem is that a back porch, and most of the other places where you do your testing, are usually protected from the wind. Your stove lights without much trouble, and it builds up to its super-hot blue-green flame, and everybody feels jolly all over. You can hardly wait to get it into the woods and to heat up a freeze-dried bouillabaisse.

All too often, when you do get it into the woods, you discover that one important element was missing from that back-porch test: a good stiff breeze, or perhaps a fresh gale. Now, in the wilderness, it comes up the valley and into your encampment, and it aims directly at the burner head of your stove, and with what seems like the slightest of puffs it turns the blue-green flame into a feeble wisp of orange or yellow. The time it takes to boil your water suddenly doubles and triples. You arrange your windscreen, if one came with the stove, and you shift your position so that your body will block most of the wind. Then the wind starts coming from the other direction.

The Peak 1 suffers less from these problems than any other backpacking stove I know. The reason is an insignificant-looking windscreen, which also supports the pot. The windscreen is made in the shape of an X, which apparently breaks the wind up into four quadrants. A strong breeze might affect the flames coming from one quadrant, but the other three hum along merrily, still providing the heat you need.

Why, you might well ask, has there been no mention so far of the Svea 123, certainly the backpacking world's favorite stove? The one that Colin Fletcher called "a wonderful little stove" and referred to as "Fifteen years my trusted friend"? The stove that *Backpacker* magazine termed "probably . . . the most popular backpacking stove for the largest time," one that "has developed a cult of loyal followers who put up with its eccentricities with an affectionate sentimentality"?

There is little discussion here of the Svea, and no comparative test information, because the ones I have dealt with have turned out to be absolute turkeys. The Svea did to me what a backpacking stove should never do: It failed me. Failed me utterly and completely and left me hungry.

And I am not exaggerating when I say "utterly and completely": The Svea, a brand-new one but one that had tested out okay at home, broke down on me at the very beginning of a week-long expedition to a primitive island off the coast of Georgia. Because the breakdown occurred at the beginning, I was forced to eat a great deal of uncooked backpacking food, and I was further forced to abstain, for the first time since I was a teen-ager, from coffee in the morning. (That, I thought, was the cruelest blow imaginable. Since then, however, I have managed to eliminate coffee almost completely from my diet, and it didn't hurt at all.)

The breakdown was in the mechanism that regulates the Svea's fuel mixture. It allowed pressure to escape so that the stove could not generate any real heat. When I returned to the mainland, I went back to the store that had sold me the Svea—a reputable backpacking shop. They took a look at the faulty mechanism, pronounced it the victim of sloppy factory work, and gave me a new Svea.

The new machine certainly generated real heat. Big, flaming, frightening balls of it. It soon developed that the only way to make it *stop* acting like the ending of a James Bond chase scene was to clap a pot over it and deprive it of oxygen. The reputable backpacking shop, by now tired of my whining, made a half-hearted attempt to solve the problem, then gave up, leaving me with 20-some-bucks' worth of dangerous backpacking stove. At that point I said to hell with the Svea 123. Some of us are just not cut out to be cult followers. I went back to my Optimus 99.*

* All right, ready for the kicker? The Optimus and the Svea are made by the same company, the same people, and possibly in the same building. There is no rational basis for

So much, then, for the machines at the center of the backpacker's kitchen. None of the stoves currently available is perfect, although I think the Peak 1 comes closest. All of them employ trade-offs of one sort or another: Spastic operation or slow boiling times are often the prices you pay for extreme light weight. Butane stoves are easy to operate, but the fuel they use presents a problem. New contenders are coming on the market all the time, and I suggest you take their advertising claims with a pound of salt tablets and see what the reputable testers, such as the people at *Backpacker*, say about them.†

•

There's more that should find its way into your backpacker's kitchen. But not *too* much. Too much here, as elsewhere in your pack, will mean too much weight on your back, and that, of course, is what you want to avoid. What follows is, again, what works best for me, and should be interpreted as merely a set of suggestions.

Fuel tanks. If your stove runs on butane, you won't need these, of course. You'll just need to re-

---

anyone, including me, to despise one and cherish the other. But it happens all the time. The woods are probably full (literally) of people who have had no trouble at all with their Sveas but had equally horrible experiences with an Optimus.

† A relatively recent entry, for instance, is the MSR stove, developed and sold by the Mountain Safety Research people in Seattle. It is one of the oddest stoves made, with a circle of what looks like tinfoil for a windscreen and a metal plate that you place on the burner in order to get a simmer. But everybody who's tested it agrees it is a supremely hot stove. It also costs something like $45, which I consider obscene.

member to carry out of the woods all those butane canisters you emptied.

If you use gasoline, though, you'll need efficient, dependable containers in which to carry your extra supply. How much extra, nobody knows; it depends on the sort of food you cook (do you just boil water, or do you do elaborate cooking?), how often you cook (it's possible to live perfectly well in the woods with cold meals for both breakfast and lunch —and even dinner as well), and the sort of stove you have.

The best fuel containers I know are made of anodized spun aluminum by Sigg, of Switzerland. Watch out for imitators. With the Siggs I use a specially made cap that allows you to pour a controlled, small stream of fuel into your stove's tank without too much mess. You'll spill some, but not as much as usual. The special cap can't be left on the fuel bottle all the time, of course; I attach it to the regular cap with a short length of cord.

Potgrabber. If your cooking pots had handles projecting from their sides, they'd take up too much room. But you need something to shuffle them around with. The small aluminum potgrabber, which is sort of like a pair of pliers, is ideal for this. The one that comes with the Optimus 99 is the smallest I've seen, and it works as efficiently as the larger ones. Potgrabbers come with several cooksets, and they may be bought individually.

Even smaller, almost as efficient, and useful for other jobs as well is a tiny pair of ignition pliers, available at hardware and automotive stores.

I also carry a cheap, lightweight pair of cotton work gloves, colored red so I can find them easily. They're great for handling hot cooking utensils and stoves, and on more than one occasion I have worn them through a night that turned out to be colder than I expected.

Pots and pans. Or maybe, if you're traveling alone and really light, it should read just "pot." It must be large enough to boil all the water you need, small enough to take backpacking. I find the Sigg spun aluminum pot to be the best. It has a bail handle that ordinarily doesn't become too hot. There's a lid that can be used as a lid, as a plate, or as a frying pan (if you're very careful. The aluminum is quite thin, and it's easy to burn something).

The Siggs come in three sizes, from 1½ to 3½ quarts. They can nest together, and while you're traveling you can pack a lot of other kitchen gear inside them, or it. Some stoves will fit inside.

If you're really interested in traveling light, and alone, and you aren't planning any elaborate meals, you might be interested in the Optimus 126 cookset. This is a nest of three small aluminum pots, the largest about 5½ inches in diameter, that hold from about 12 to 22 ounces of liquid. There is a pot-grabber and an insubstantial plastic drinking cup. The top of the nest is said to double as a frying pan, but it has heavy concentric circles scribed into it, and I imagine it would be difficult to use for something like eggs or pancakes. But the small size of the package might interest you. The cookset weighs just a little over 6 ounces.

Another contender is the cookset that is made by Campways. Billed as an outfit for two persons, it consists of a 1½-quart pot and a Teflon-coated pan that fits over the pot and that can be used as its lid. Inside are two plates, a pot scrubber, and two plastic 8-ounce drinking cups.

I find the Campways set especially helpful when

there's frying or bread-cooking to be done. The Teflon pan, which is sort of a cross between a saucepan and a skillet, works better than a Sigg lid for making pancakes or frying fish.

I use the plastic cup that comes with the Campways, but when I'm camping alone I leave the plates behind. One person really doesn't need such refinements in the woods. One of the plates may be handy, though, as a surface for mixing dough or some other material that has an affinity for pine needles and ants.

Spoon. Also among the refinements that you don't need are a fork or a dinner-type knife. The aluminum spoon that came in one of those cheap backpacking utensil sets that I bought years ago, when I didn't know any better, serves now as my sole eating implement. It is rather large, holds one tablespoon, and has been sawed off by me with a hacksaw so that it fits neatly into the Campways cookset.

The spoon came with two tiny rivet-like gizmos on its shank. They were used to make it join together with the fork and knife. Now I find that the gizmo that remains, after my attack with the hacksaw, is useful for hanging the spoon on the side of a pot or pan; it keeps the utensil from sliding into my stew.

Knife. This is more of a cooking than an eating utensil. Some people still go into the woods wearing sheath knives big enough to mince redwoods, but they're not at all necessary. I use a knife that folds, and that therefore can be called a pocket knife, but that is rather large when it's unfolded, and that therefore can be called a hunting knife. It's made by Gerber; open it is 8 inches long, closed it's 4½. A lock keeps it from doubling back on my hand when it's open.

I find that knife suitable for any cutting chore that

comes up except mustache-trimming,* and that includes shaving meat bars into soup, slicing cheese, and filleting fish.

Can opener. If you eat nothing but the freeze-dried delicacies you get at backpacking stores, you may never need a can opener. If you follow the recipes in this book, you will. I have tried to find a small, lightweight can opener, and have had to settle for a small but frustrating item called the Ekco Miracle Roll Can Opener. It's just a couple of inches long, weighs very little, and costs 69 cents.

But it's frustrating. And if you're going to have frustration anyway, you might as well use the original GI can opener, which is so small you have to tie something to it to keep from losing it, and which weighs practically nothing.

Water bottles. Water will be the most important thing you will consume, so it stands to reason that you should make proper arrangements for carrying it safely. There are dozens of sizes and shapes of plastic bottles and bags, and the number and size you carry depend on how scarce your drinking water will be. It may even be necessary, as it was for me once on an uninhabited island off North Carolina, to cache water for future use.

In that case, I stored a 5-gallon container, made of heavy but flexible plastic, under a bush, along with a note about whom it was for and when I would be using it—and a request that the finder leave it alone. Nobody did find it before I got to it, at a time when my traveling water supply was low, but my joy was tempered by the fact that the plastic

---

* For that I use a tiny pair of folding scissors, having discovered years ago that the scissors on my Swiss army knife were next to worthless.

bag apparently had acted as a magnifying lens, and the water inside was quite hot. Next time, I'll bury the bag in the sand.

I have found that it's quite helpful to carry along a quart-sized plastic water container that is shaped like a milk bottle and that has a fairly wide mouth. I use it for mixing fake fruit-juice drinks and the like, and when I have to collect water with my drinking cup from a tiny trickle, the wide mouth makes it easier to pour the water in.

Drinking and measuring cup. I see no harm in the Sierra Club stainless-steel cup. I belong to the club and support its work. Many people, frustrated because the nature of the sport denies them an official backpacking uniform, and made uneasy by the fact that ranks and badges and classifications of expertise cannot yet be assigned to people who walk in the woods, quite naturally *need* something like the Sierra Club cup as proof that they are Experts.

The cup has its uses, such as for boiling just one cup of water for coffee or tea, but I much prefer to use the cheap and unstatusy plastic cup that comes with many cooksets. You can't boil water in it, but its great advantage is that it is clearly marked, on the inside where it counts, in $\frac{1}{4}$, $\frac{1}{2}$, $\frac{3}{4}$, and 1-cup gradations. So you use it for cooking as well as for eating and drinking. Palco is one of those who makes the cups.

Tiny Austrian bottles. These are polyethylene containers with wide mouths and chunky green caps that are easy to open and close, and they are useful in dozens of ways, including the carrying of salt, pepper, honey, soy sauce, herbs, and spices. Three sizes that I use most are $3\frac{1}{2}$, $2\frac{3}{4}$, and $2\frac{1}{4}$ inches tall.

Note that I spoke of salt and pepper. I have been unable, after much experimentation and waste of money, to find a backpacking salt-and-pepper container that is worthy of the name. Most of them leak. The Austrian bottles don't leak, and the lack of some sort of shaker mechanism doesn't bother me at all.

Other containers. It's likely that you will be carrying margarine with you, and it's almost certain that you will have a supply of peanut butter. Some campers use Gerry Tubes, which are like toothpaste tubes except they are made of plastic and are open at both ends; you spoon in your peanut butter, or whatever, and then slide a plastic crimping device over one end to seal it. The other end is covered with a conventional screw cap.

I have had less than complete success with Gerry Tubes, and I prefer to carry such foodstuffs in small, round freezer containers, found at housewares and dime stores. The ones that have worked best for me are called Superseal Food Saver Jars. They come, by the way, with marketing labels that are easily removed once you get home from the store, rather than with stickers you have to attack with solvent and a power sander. The jars in larger sizes are also useful for storing, between expeditions and at home, items such as dried milk, quick rice, and so forth.

Plastic bags. People born since the Forties probably assume that Baggies, like ball-point pens and television, were around forever, but they weren't. And it is amazing how much of an impact the small plastic bag has made on backpacking. The bags weigh virtually nothing; they do a reasonably good job of containing whatever's in them (especially if you double-bag the really troublesome items); they show what's inside; they're easy to pack out. They are very helpful.

Some hikers like Ziploc Storage Bags, which sort of "zip" closed under fingernail pressure. I find that the zipper channel has a tendency to get clogged up with certain substances, such as instant coffee or tea or, especially, fake-fruit powders.

Heavier bags, which are not as universally available, are very good for wrapping up cooksets (and keeping soot from spreading within your pack) and stoves and generally sorting out heavier and bulkier items. At different times and in different places, I have been able to find the stronger bags at aquariums (they put fish in them, remember?), at "party" stores that have bag-it-yourself ice machines, and in bait-and-tackle shops, particularly those situated along salt water.

Matches. I always carry several books of them, in various places throughout my pack, on the theory that if one gets wet and ruined, the others might not. I have a small ditty bag that I call my "repair bag," which contains emergency stuff (a piece of wire, spare flashlight batteries, a little bit of plastic tape), and in that bag I also carry my most secure spare matches—three books wrapped several times in plastic film and then sealed with cellophane tape.

Insulating platform for the stove. This is the aforementioned piece of closed-cell foam that I put under the stove to insulate and steady it. I cut it from a larger, scrap piece; it's about 9 by 12 inches by ⅜ inch thick, and I chose those dimensions because they fit neatly into the top flap of my backpack. The pad is useful all the time, most so when I wake up after an all-night rain, open the fly-screen of my tent, and start to manipulate the little stove into life.

It's the difference between doing it in mud and doing it on a dry, firm surface.

The mention of mud brings up the subject of sanitation, which is every bit as important in the woods as it is in a city apartment or a suburban ranch house—perhaps more so, since sickness brought on by insanitary conditions could cause serious problems for a solitary backpacker.

Our tendency is to think, correctly, of the wilderness as a clean place, much cleaner than the filthy city streets. But sometimes we forget about making sure that we, ourselves, are clean. Hot running water is rather rare in the woods, so we tend to forget to wash our hands after excreting and/or before cooking. This can lead to a rather instant case of the runs, and that can spoil a trip. So it's wise to think of sanitation and hygiene as part and parcel of the backpacker's kitchen. Following are some of the items you might want to carry along:

Soap. Here, as elsewhere in backpacking, it's helpful if you can make one item do several different jobs. In this case, you'd like your soap to be useful not just for washing dishes, but also for washing yourself and your clothes. Some soaps made specially for backpackers are supposed to do all this—and even clean your teeth as well—but they work out costing something like $12 a pint, which explains why they're sold in such small quantities.

You might want to try some old-fashioned liquid detergent, which does everything *except* brush your teeth. I use Ivory Liquid Gentle White Detergent, which comes from the supermarket in the usual large container. I decant the stuff into a small plastic bottle from the dime store which has a spout top that can be easily opened and closed. The bottle is wrapped up in a small Baggie for traveling and put, with the following item, inside my cooking pot.

Scrub brush or pad. The one that I've found to be best is the Chore Reddy Cleaning Puff, which is a roundish, yellow thing. It is safe for Teflon-coated utensils and is supposed to be "fingernail safe," whatever that might be.

Purification tablets. It's wise to carry some, even if you *think* the water's clean. I find that water subjected to the tablets doesn't taste all that bad, especially if you shake it and get a lot of oxygen into it. The ones I use are known as Coughlan's Emergency Drinking Water Germicidal Tablets, and they do their stuff with iodine. Be sure to read the instructions *before* you set out for the woods, so you understand the tablets' limitations. And be sure to write down the chemical's expiration date on the label.

Towel and washcloth. Go to a dime store and buy a cheap washcloth and face towel with plenty of absorbency and in the most garish color imaginable (so you won't lose them and so they won't get included in the general supply at home). Keep them in a plastic bag, but remember to dry them out when you make camp.

Some other items, more related to personal hygiene than the kitchen.
You may want to carry some folded, foil-wrapped moist towels. A child's toothbrush (smaller, lighter, and almost as efficient as an adult one) is handy, along with an Austrian bottle full of baking soda (for tooth-cleaning, fire-extinguishing, and many other uses). Small, compact rolls of biodegradable toilet paper are available. A 2-ounce, plastic, but strong backpacker's trowel helps to dig mini-latrines

and may be obtained from Recreational Equipment, Inc.

And no paper towels. It's amazing how we Americans, who have been trained to go through at least a half a roll of paper towels a day, and to amuse ourselves during the evening hours by watching professional models gush over them in TV commercials, can find, after even the shortest outing in the woods, that they aren't really necessary at all.

Garbage bags. They *are* extremely necessary, because you're going to have stuff to pack out of the woods. And remember, if you're really nice you're even going to pick up other people's messes on your way out. The bags that fit into kitchen-type garbage cans, and that claim to hold 4½ gallons, are about the right size.

That's about all you'll need to prepare food on the trail. If you want to do a complete job of packaging it at home, you can go a little further:

Scale. It's not at all necessary, but it helps in determining portions, and it's useful elsewhere at home. I don't trust scales with springs nearly as much as those with beam balances.

Measuring cup. The graduated one from your backpack will do fine.

Measuring spoon. The 1-tablespoon eating utensil mentioned earlier has been entirely adequate.

Boilable cooking pouches. These are heavy-duty plastic pouches in various sizes ("small," for instance, is about 6 by 8 inches and holds 8 fluid ounces) that may be sealed by heat, and that thus are much better than ordinary Baggies at keeping air and moisture out. These pouches are found in housewares departments of big stores; the Sears, Roebuck brand is called Meals in Minutes, for example, and Dazey makes one called Seal a Meal. Most manufacturers would have you buy a special heat-sealing device, at $10 to $20, to close the bags. It's not necessary, though. All you need is a soldering iron with a plastic-melting tip (Weller makes one). Or an ordinary flat iron, plus a little experimentation, will do.

Instructions. Inside each bag that contains a meal or a component of a meal, you'll need to put a piece of paper with clearly written instructions as to how to cook the meal. Ordinarily this means just a word or two about what the dish is (sometimes you can't tell from looking at them), and the notation to "boil 8 oz. water, add contents, stir, eat" or something similar.

And, of course, you'll need the food.

4

SOME BASIC FOODS

The backpacker who uses the recipes in this book, and who establishes her or his own system, is probably going to accumulate quickly a list of basic, stock ingredients that fit his or her own particular needs and appetites. To a large extent, the ingredients are interchangeable, and because of this the average, recreational backpacker should never have to worry about a lack of variety in the trail kitchen.

The list that has evolved in my case goes like this:

Starches. By and large, this means rice, mashed potatoes, noodles, and pasta. By themselves, these starches would provide an awfully unsatisfying diet, not to mention an unhealthy one. But they are extremely helpful, in conjunction with protein, vegetables, and liquids, in constructing simple trail meals, particularly those that are cooked in one pot.

Whole societies, as everybody knows, live almost exclusively off a diet of rice and some sort of beans, and that has led some observers to conclude that rice is some sort of a wonder food. If you're of that inclination, I suggest you dig up the July, 1976, copy of *Consumer Reports*. The magazine acknowledges, in a comprehensive article on the food, that rice is "a good, inexpensive extender" for meat and poultry, but adds that it is lacking in important nutrients.

So don't go into the woods with only a sack of rice. Rice does provide, though, a very good, tasty, and filling complement for meats and other sources of protein, and its small grains are excellent for absorbing and transporting tastes through a soup or a stew, which much backpacking food ends up being.

Backpackers who use rice almost always choose the "instant" or "quick" varieties, which taste nowhere near as good as the regular kind, but which cook in much less time, saving a good deal of fuel. For years I used nothing but Minute Rice, made by General Foods, in trail cooking, and I always felt resentful at the huge difference in taste between it and the rice I cooked at home. The word that inevitably came to my mind when I bit into Minute Rice was "cardboard."

Then I discovered Uncle Ben's Quick Rice. This rice *looks*, when you open the box, like cardboard. It is puffy and decidedly unattractive-looking. But it tastes much better, in my estimation, than Minute.*

Mashed potatoes are another excellent binder for backpacking dishes, although perhaps less versatile than rice. Or at least *I* think they're less versatile. Not the marketing people. Borden, on the side of its Country Store brand, urges you to put the product on scalloped corn, macaroni and cheese, green beans, cauliflower, broiled tomatoes, carrots,

---

* In the recipes that follow that employ rice, I am setting forth a volume of water sufficient to cook Uncle Ben's. If you use Minute or another brand, you will need to make adjustments in the amount of water, which is fairly critical in rice cookery. Minute's instructions call for using equal volumes of rice and water, while Uncle Ben's call for less water. Particularly in cooking quick rice, experimentation is needed to determine the consistency that you prefer.

and asparagus. Worst of all, "Let the family help themselves right at the table from a bowl of toasted Country Store Mashed Potato Flakes. . . . Over ice-cream—a nut-like flavor. . . . Try it on tossed salad."

All this is very silly, but I recently had occasion to conduct an in-depth survey of uncooked mashed potato flakes. That was when I was on the island with my unspeakable busted Svea stove. Quite a few of the meals I had packaged utilized mashed potatoes as their starch, and I found myself eating the stuff raw.

It wasn't all that bad. It tasted a bit like the super-bland baby cereal that one used to swipe from one's younger siblings. Then I tried mixing cold water with the flakes and eating that. It wasn't so bad, either. At least it was better than eating uncooked quick rice.

The last two starches, pasta and noodles, require considerably more water to prepare than do rice and mashed potatoes. This might be an important consideration if you're hiking in places where water is scarce.

Noodles, which are usually made from eggs and flour, take up more room in your pack than other starches, but they provide a taste and texture that can be really satisfying at the end of a tiring day. Pasta, which includes spaghetti and macaroni and comes from hard wheat, takes up less room, unless you're into fancy seashells and curlicues, and also makes its distinctive contributions in the area of taste and texture, especially when tomato sauce is involved.

When buying pasta, you might want to check the instructions to determine the boiling time. Manufacturers vary, sometimes considerably, in the times they require. Buitoni, for instance, says 5 to 9 minutes for some of its products; Ronzoni says 12 to 15. Both are delicious. But you'll have to carry less fuel if you use Buitoni.

I will probably be accused of gross ingratitude by my Italian-American neighbors for saying this, but the best backpacking pasta I have found yet is something called Creamettes that is made by somebody called The Creamette Company in, of all places, Minneapolis. Creamettes cook in 6 to 8 minutes at sea level, they are compact enough so they don't take up a lot of room, and (maybe this is my imagination, or maybe I'm being hypnotized by their name) they taste *creamier* than other pasta.

Protein. We all know we must have this so our bodies might continue the lifelong process of rebuilding themselves. The amino acids that go into proteins, and which the body must have, are found, as we all have been taught since grammar school, in eggs, milk, fish, and meat—all of them foodstuffs that backpackers might find difficult to conveniently carry on the trail, but that must, nevertheless, be carried.

Protein of a less complete quality—that is, without some or enough of the important aminos—is also found in nuts, grains, seeds, and legumes. And here we could enter—but won't—the never-ending discussion of animal meat versus vegetarianism, a discussion that is every bit as controversial, for some people, as religion or politics.*

The protein-laden foods that figure in this list include canned tuna, turkey, chicken, shrimp, Vienna sausage, and other frequently uninspiring delicacies

---

* The classic book that argues for "high-protein meatless cooking" is Frances Moore Lappé's *Diet for a Small Planet* (Ballantine, 1975 revised edition), which may almost universally be found in paperback in "health-food" stores.

from the supermarket; some meat products from the backpacking-supply stores; and, peanuts, soybeans, and cashews.

Tuna fish, like baked beans, is one of those things you see almost exclusively in a can, rather than in its "homemade" or "fresh" condition. It is a standard component of sandwiches, casseroles, salads, loaves, and even pies. Entire suburban families subsist on it for weeks at a time. A whole new wing of the food-selling industry has been founded on providing a "helper" for tuna—to make it taste a little different, or to extend it so that money may be allegedly saved.

Fortunately for the backpacker, tuna comes in containers compact enough to be carried on the trail. The standard size for a solitary hiker is the 3½-ounce can. That weight refers to the amount of food inside; the can itself weighs almost another ounce. Inside, with the tuna, is some water or oil, salt, and the usual strange-sounding chemical or two.

Some backpackers might not want to include tuna in their master list of foodstuffs until the American tuna fleet exhibits more of a desire to end its routine slaughter of dolphins, with whom the yellowfin tuna travels.

Boned turkey and chicken come in cans that are a little larger and heavier than the tuna—a net weight of 5 ounces is standard—and they are usually packed in a broth. While the stuff that comes out of a tuna can registers on our taste buds as "tuna" because few of us have tasted fresh tuna, the reverse is often true with canned poultry. We're used to eating fresh, or relatively fresh, chicken and turkey, and so the canned variety tends to be tasteless and without the proper texture. The solution to this, as with many problems of backpacking gourmandism, is to rely on a good day of walking to build an appetite that can ignore such subtle, and not-so-subtle, distinctions.

Canned shrimps, in containers ranging from 4½ to 9 ounces in weight (half that represents the drained weight of the shrimps), are the least successful of the canned proteins, mostly because the shrimps are small ones, and they are soggy. They tend to get lost in whatever you're cooking. It helps to buy the largest-sized shrimps available, to drain the juice in which they're packed (and, if possible, to soak them in cold water before using), and to add them to the pot only at the end of the cooking period, with a minimum of stirring. (The shrimps, along with the other canned meats and poultry, are already cooked when you open the can.)

Some people hate Vienna sausages. Some love them. I'm ambivalent, but I always wonder while I'm eating them what they're made of. Their chief advantage and attractiveness to the backpacker is the fact that they come in small, 5-ounce cans. They can be added to soups, stews, and pasta-and-cheese dishes, or may be eaten from the can for lunch. It would be much nicer, however, if they tasted better.

The protein stockpile is increased by several megatons if you allow yourself the luxury of an occasional freeze-dried meat of the sort that is available at backpacking stores. The grandparent of all these is the Campsite Freeze Dry Meat Bar, packed by Wilson & Company. The bar weighs about 3 ounces, comes wrapped in foil inside a cardboard package that is about 3¼ by 2 by 1 inch, needs no refrigeration, and is composed of compressed beef and pork.

It is possible to simply chew on a meat bar as it comes out of the box (and backpackers who like to prepare for any eventuality are often found carrying one, along with matches and a whistle and other items, in their emergency kits). You have to be careful not to eat the cardboard package as well, since it and the meat taste about the same. You might have more fun if you use the bar in soups or stews.

Wilson also makes a similarly sized Bacon Bar, which is freeze-dried, pressed, and pre-fried bacon (along with all the usual chemicals that processors like to put in pork), which has similar uses. The meat and bacon bars sell for $2.15 to $2.50 each.

The more complete backpacking stores are likely to have other freeze-dried meats in one- or two-person portions (as opposed to selling them as constituents of larger meals such as "Tuna à la Neptune" and "Beef Almondine"), and you may want to work them into your menus. Ham, chicken, beef, and meatballs are frequently available.

Such meats are relatively easy to prepare. Wilson's Certified Freeze-Dried Ham, for example, comes in a tiny 1-ounce can. The manufacturer asks that you open the can, fill it with water, let it stand for 10 minutes, drain it, and add the contents to whatever dish you're making. The result is something that tastes pretty much like ham but doesn't have ham's texture. The packers manage to throw in some gristle, though.

Some backpacking stores also sell vegetable protein concoctions, made up of soybean flour and other things, that are alleged to be flavored like meats and poultry. I have not tried these and I hope I never have to.

In meats and poultry, as elsewhere, new items are coming on the market all the time, and the imaginative backpacker will want to consider adding new entries to the list. But read the label, and test the product at home first. One item I would *not* add to the list is something that appeared, accompanied by large newspaper advertisements, during 1976. It was called Tender Chunk Ham.

The obvious intention of the manufacturer of this stuff was to associate it in the shopper's mind with that safe and reliable old standby, tuna fish. The advertisements told people to look for it next to the tuna, and the label says you can use it "just like tuna." The cans weighed in at about 6¾ ounces (a little less than the weight of a standard tuna can) and cost 89 cents, which equals about $2.10 a pound. Inside was a pinkish mass (the label, possibly anticipating our reaction upon seeing it for the first time, has assured us that it is "real ham") that tasted, to me, about the way it looked, which was not like ham at all, but like *processing.* I suspect we're in for a lot more of this type of treatment in the years to come.

The sources of protein that are not meat are easily obtainable. The ones I use are peanuts, cashews, and soybean nuts, but the list could be much longer. When I started writing this book, I was prepared to advocate the use of peanuts and the like as trail snacks, but I hardly thought of them as main ingredients of the one-pot dinner. I experimented with them, however, at the suggestion of my roommate, the intuitive person, and now I am able to report that my all-time favorite backpacking dish is a curry that is built around peanuts.

Vegetables. They are valuable, of course, for carbohydrates and vitamins, but they also serve to provide the varied, and several, tastes that are helpful in a one-pot meal. One obvious, lightweight, and convenient source for these vegetables is dried soup mixes. When rehydrated, usually with less water than they would require if they were to serve just as soups, they turn the dinner mixture into something approximating more of a stew. And they add additional tastes—tomato, carrot, green pepper, onion—to a dish that otherwise might boast just two flavors, such as rice and beef.

The soup mixes to which I am most indebted are those that go under the name of Cup-a-Soup. They are manufactured by Thomas J. Lipton, Inc. and come in a variety of flavors, the major ones being tomato, cream of mushroom, onion, and vegetable variations. Occasionally new flavors are introduced and others withdrawn.*

The soups are packaged in foil envelopes, each weighing about ½ ounce, and they come four to a box. Each envelope, if it were used to make soup, would combine with 6 ounces (not a cup) of hot water. The process is as quick as making instant coffee.

Lipton also makes a line of soups, in slightly larger envelopes, that require simmering for five minutes or so. These, too, are very useful. Often you'll find that the ingredients in them have more character— they're less pulverized than the instant soups, which must dissolve more quickly.

Other brands of instant soups are on the market, too, and you might want to experiment with them. The Nestlé Company makes something that looks very much like an imitation of Cup-a-Soup, called Souptime. The list of ingredients is staggering: It is full of chemicals and very low on what I would call

---

* One that was taken off the market, and that would have figured nicely into several of these recipes, was lobster bisque. And there was cream of asparagus, which seemed to hang around all of two weeks before it disappeared from the supermarket shelves.

"natural" ingredients. There is more salt in the company's French onion soup than there are onions.

Nestlēs' cream of chicken soup is even scarier, with an array of chemicals that makes my mind boggle and my stomach wince. It is not surprising that Nestlē changed the name of this contrivance in 1976 from Cream of Chicken Soup to Cream of Chicken Flavor Soup.

Some people might want to experiment with dehydrated soup greens, which are available in some supermarkets and which vary widely in price. These usually contain tomatoes, carrots, celery, onions, and perhaps green peppers. They take somewhat more time to rehydrate than do the more finely ground soup mixes, and they taste about the same.

As mentioned earlier in this book, freeze-dried green peas are also included on the basic list. The taste they impart to a one-pot dinner makes them worth the elevated price you have to pay for them.

Dried milk is frequently used in backpacking recipes. The kind I use is the kind most frequently encountered in the supermarket: instant nonfat dry milk, fortified with vitamins A and D, extra grade. That last designation is supposed to mean that the milk powder is easier to dissolve in water.

There are a couple of other forms of dry milk, most often found in "health-food" stores: nonfat, noninstant milk; and whole, noninstant, which contains more butterfat. Both are more difficult to reconstitute than instant nonfat milk.

Cheese is a good source of protein, and it keeps well except in the hottest weather. It packs a good deal of nourishment and satisfaction for its weight. Generally speaking, the harder the cheese, the better it will travel. You also might want to use dried, prepackaged cheese products, which weigh less, keep very well, and take up less room, but which are not, strictly speaking, officially cheeses. An example would be A&P's Grated American Cheese Food, which is sold in cardboard containers with shaker tops and which requires no refrigeration. The product is made up of cheddar cheese that has been aged, dried, and grated, and dry milk, cheese whey solids, salt, sodium phosphate, and artificial coloring.

Fats for cooking and/or flavoring are not absolutely essential, but they are convenient and enhance taste. If you're carrying margarine (which is easily done except in highest temperatures) to add flavor to your stews or to make your mashed potatoes more palatable, you won't need any oil to cook with. Just use margarine.

If you do want to carry cooking oil, select one with a taste (or lack of taste) that will blend with all the dishes in which you use it. Olive oil, for instance, might be fine for a spaghetti dish but a little too assertive for scrambled eggs. I have found peanut oil to be as close to all-purpose as anything.

Once I heard about a cooking oil that was supposed to be flavored like butter, and I could not rest until I found and tried some. Don't waste your time on it.

Vegaline is a product, sold in backpacking stores, that does the job of oils in preventing foods from sticking to the pan. Two or three drops are all that are required to coat a pan, so you need to carry along only a 1-ounce container of the stuff. It is made partly of lecithin, a phosphorous-containing substance.

And then there's a whole category of items that may be described more accurately as *flavors* than as foods. They're tiny and lightweight and generally inexpensive, and often they can make the difference between a meal that's as bland as kindergarten tapioca and one that's interesting. Dried mushrooms, which used to be found only in specific ethnic enclaves such as Chinese neighborhoods, are now appearing in suburban supermarkets. Instant tea and coffee (or, in the case of tea, the real stuff in bags or bulk) also fall into this category.

Supermarkets are full of little envelopes containing gravy, sauce, and other sorts of mixes, many of which just combine with a small quantity of water, cook a few minutes, and are ready to use. If you're tempted to experiment with some of the more exotic ones, such as hollandaise sauce or oriental sweet-and-sour sauce, by all means do. But be prepared for a letdown. There's a limit, after all, to what can be done with hydrolyzed vegetable protein and whey solids.

Bouillon and broth cubes and packets bring flavor to stews. Any grocery store has them in the three most popular flavors—beef, chicken, and vegetable. In choosing these tiny, concentrated doses of flavor, as in all the other shopping you'll be doing, read the fine print on the labels. Some broths manage to achieve their chicken flavor without very much association with a chicken at all; others at least let a retired rooster walk through the pot.

Many flavors can be transported in the small Austrian plastic jars that were described in the preceding chapter. These would include soy sauce, sherry for cooking (alcohol and plastic are never close friends; drain the sherry and clean the jar between trips); honey (it seems to be able to find its way out of any container; you may need to lick the jar every once in a while); salt and pepper; dried flakes of green pepper and celery or celery salt.

Dried onions come in a variety of consistencies,

from a fine powder to coarse but lightweight flakes that rehydrate into something almost approximating onions. The same can be said of dried garlic. Garlic, though, is compact, powerful, and lightweight even in its natural form; you might want to just pack away a few cloves of the stuff and peel and slice it as you travel.

Herbs and spices (spices are from the tropics, herbs from temperate climates) go well in the Austrian jars or wrapped up in small bits of plastic film. Some common, and welcome, ones include parsley, rosemary, chives, basil, oregano, bay leaf, coriander, cumin, chili powder, and dry mustard.

And you can manufacture your own mixtures of herbs and spices: your own curry mixture or a store-bought one; a combination of herbs that taste especially good in Italian dishes; some commercial poultry seasoning (itself a mixture of sage, oregano, ginger, rosemary, marjoram, thyme, pepper, and celery seed) for use in dishes involving chicken or turkey and for experimentation in other foods. I like to make up a jar of what I call Creole mix, which is not totally authentic but which passes the back-packing test: small amounts of dried cayenne pepper, bay leaf, basil, rosemary, thyme, filé, marjoram, savory, mace, brown sugar, garlic, onions, green pepper, and celery.

Herb books, of which there are several on the market, can help you decide which flavors and smells to experiment with. Like adding sage to macaroni and cheese and seeing what happens. Or chives to scrambled eggs.

Many spices and herbs are available in supermarkets, of course. Some of the more exotic ones, usually at equally exotic prices, may be found in "gourmet" sections of department stores or in some "health-food" stores. (The Spice Market, at 265

Canal Street, New York City, 10013, does a mail-order business in dozens or herbs and allied items. They have, for instance, not one but five types of dried mushrooms.)

Some flavors cost a good deal. Others cost practically nothing, and dedicated backpackers who are also on the cheap make certain that they take advantage of such "free" offers.

I'm referring to the little packets of mustard and ketchup you may fail to ask for when you get a fast-food hamburger, and the capsules of soy sauce, mustard sauce, and duck sauce that come with a Chinese take-out meal. One of the dishes described on the following pages, potato pancakes, is one of my favorites when I'm seized with a carbohydrate attack. It's kind of messy to mix up the pancake batter, and the pan's a little hard to clean afterwards, but the rewards of eating a genuine potato pancake while lying in your sleeping bag on the side of a hill are manifold.

There was, however, always something missing. It was ketchup. I'm one of those savages who like ketchup on potatoes.

Now, it's difficult to carry ketchup on a backpacking trip. It should be refrigerated after being exposed to the air. Its inconvenience pretty much outweighs its usefulness. But then I remembered all those little packets of ketchup I had received, and not eaten, on all those long automobile trips when I had succumbed to the temptation to stop at a McDonald's or Burger King because at least I knew what I'd be getting.

I dug all the maps, tire gauges, and failed ball-point pens out of the glove compartment of the car. Sure enough, there they patiently waited: enough packets of ketchup to keep me in potato pancakes from Maine to Georgia, if need be.

5

BREAKFAST, LUNCH, AND IN-BETWEEN

These are meals that are essential, but maybe not *as* essential as the evening meal. A backpacker spends less time on breakfast, lunch, and the inevitable snacks than she or he spends on dinner, and for obvious reasons: You're on the move, usually, in the morning and at noon. You want calories, because without them you'll become exhausted, frustrated, irritable, and depressed. But you don't want elaborate, heavy meals, nor do you want to have to spend a lot of time cleaning up after them. So they tend to be something less than gourmet romps.

Following are some recipes that seem to do the job. They provide energy for the walking, as well as some of the psychological satisfaction that a hiker needs at the beginning and middle of the day, and often during morning and afternoon breaks as well.

BREAKFAST

Instant Breakfast Drinks

For many of us, breakfast is as likely to be a liquid meal as a solid one: Coffee or tea are necessary ingredients of any plan to fully regain consciousness for the new day. Many hikers who never touch the stuff at home find themselves taking to the woods with them instant breakfast drinks. These are the dry powders that combine with water in the field to become drinks with flavors like those of oranges, grapefruit, and the like; the best-known one is Tang, made by General Foods. The manufacturers like to smother you with information about how healthful-sounding they are (Tang, says General Foods, gives you 270 percent of your minimum daily requirement of Vitamin C), but most of them feature sugar as their major ingredient. Still, they do seem to help the day get started.

Cocoa

Cocoa and hot chocolate are also favorites, especially when cold weather's involved. You can go to a backpacking-supply store and purchase one-serving packets of instant cocoa mix for a quarter each. Or you can go to the supermarket and buy similar packets for about a dime each. The procedure is simple: Empty the cocoa mix into a cup, add 6 ounces or so of water (preferably, but not necessarily, hot), stir, and drink. A typical store brand is Nestlé's Hot Cocoa Mix, which says it contains "12 One-Cup Envelopes." This is not true. The package contains twelve envelopes, each of which makes a 6-ounce, rather than a 1-cup, drink. A cup, as we all learned in grammar school, is 8 ounces.

Or you can save even more money and prepare your cocoa yourself. You can get a 10-ounce box of the real stuff for 80 cents, and although I haven't figured out how many cups of cocoa that would make, at one tablespoonful per cup, the answer must be quite a few.

REAL COCOA

1 cup water
1 tablespoon cocoa
1 tablespoon sugar (or more or less, according to
    taste)
pinch salt
½ cup instant dry milk

At home: Put the cocoa, sugar, salt, and milk together in a plastic bag and seal it.

In the field: Put the water and the cocoa mixture in a pot and cook for a few minutes over low heat. It will be done when the mixture starts bubbling up and frothing.

Cereals

Cereals, hot and cold, are a time-honored way to get moving, and they fit well into the backpacker's kitchen. All of them may be augmented with nuts, raisins, and dried apples, peaches, apricots, and the like. Those last-named fruits may be bought dried in many supermarkets and in most "health-food" stores; you may like them better if you soak them overnight in a little water, out of the reach of raccoons, then slice them into the cereal when you wake up.

COLD CEREAL

¾ cup water
½ to 1 cup of cereal (see note)
3 tablespoons (almost ¼ cup) instant dry milk
sugar, if needed

At home: Put the cereal and dry milk, and sugar, if desired, into a plastic bag and seal.

In the field: Pour the water into the bag, stir to reconstitute the milk, and eat.

NOTE: Just about any dry cereal that will work at home will work here. I, and a number of other hikers I know, like to use Grape-Nuts as a back-packing cereal because the wheat-barley mixture is quite dense; it takes up very little room relative to its ability to fill your stomach. Granolas and the mass-produced cereals that allege themselves to be "natural" work especially well here. As is often the case with reconstituting dry milk, the colder the water is, the better the milk will taste. Because everything is contained within the plastic bag, there is no cleanup at all, beyond licking the spoon thoroughly.

LAZY OATMEAL

⅔ cup water
1 1-ounce packet of Instant Quaker Oatmeal, any flavor
1 tablespoon instant dry milk

At home: Open the oatmeal packet and pour the contents and the dry milk into a boilable plastic bag. Seal.

In the field: Bring the water to a boil, pour into the plastic bag, and stir. Wait 1 or 2 minutes and eat. Makes one serving; for heavy hiking, you may want two.

NOTE: The instant oatmeal already has salt and sugar in it. This meal, although a hot one, does not leave any dirty pots or pans.

MORE STRENUOUS, BUT ALSO
MORE REAL, OATMEAL

1 cup water
½ cup rolled oats
dash salt
sugar, if desired

At home: Package everything but the water in a plastic bag.

In the field: Bring water to a boil in a cooking pot; stir in the oats. Turn heat down to low or simmer, stirring frequently to keep oats from sticking to pot. The cereal will be done in 4 or 5 minutes. Serve as is, or add margarine, honey, raisins, and/or milk (made by dissolving 1 tablespoon instant dry milk in 4 tablespoons cold water).

NOTE: This one *does* require some cleaning up, especially if you let the oats burn to the bottom of the pot.

(A word or two here on cleaning your dishes in the woods: It's not very thoughtful to wash them in a nearby stream, nor is it necessary. Just put a little water in the pot—the hotter the better, but cold will do—and squirt in some detergent of the biodegradable sort, add your dirty utensils, soak a few minutes, and scrub like the devil with your cleaning pad or brush. So far I haven't discovered a really proper method of disposal, so I pour out the soapy water on the ground, comforted only by the fact that there's not much of it. A hot- or boiling-water rinse is necessary in order to really neutralize the harmful bacteria.)

POWERFUL OATMEAL

1 cup water
1 1-ounce packet Instant Quaker Oatmeal
3 tablespoons instant dry milk
3 tablespoons (or more, or less) condensed mincemeat

At home: Package everything but the water in a boilable plastic bag and seal.

In the field: Bring the water to a boil, pour it into the plastic bag, and stir well.

NOTE: This will give you enough energy to climb several mountains before lunch. Condensed mincemeat (Nonesuch is one brand, manufactured by Borden, Inc.) contains raisins, brown sugar, dried apples, dextrose, citrus peel, salt, currants, beef, modified starch, boiled cider, spices, distilled vinegar, caramel, vegetable oil, and artificial flavor. More than a tablespoonful or two may be too sweet for many people.

The idea for using mincemeat came from Edward B. Garvey, one of those fortunate people who have hiked the Appalachian Trail from end to end, and one of those who later wrote a book about his experiences (*Appalachian Hiker: Adventure of a Lifetime*, Appalachian Books, 1971). Garvey's excellent book contains much more information on how he managed his hike—the foods he used and consistently liked, the boots he wore, the equipment he relied on.*

Here are some strictly store-bought items that might be welcomed at breakfast time:

Cream of Wheat, that old standby, now is available in a single-serving, instant form called Mix 'n Eat. The small, 1¼-ounce packets combine with boiling water (in a cup or in a boilable plastic bag) to make a stick-to-the-ribs cereal.

* Someone who wanted to become a real backpacker could hardly do better than consult those people who have walked the Appalachian Trail, since it's more than 2,000 miles long and anybody who completes it is pretty much entitled to be called a journeyperson backpacker. Such consultation is now available via a wonderful two-volume set, *Hiking the Appalachian Trail*, edited by James R. Hare and published in 1975 by Rodale Press, Inc., Emmaus, Pennsylvania. In the books' 2,009 pages are the stories of forty-six women and men who have hiked the trail end to end. Interestingly enough, relatively few of them took along specialized backpacking food.

Cream of Rice requires less than a minute's cooking, then stands for 3 minutes before it's ready to eat.

Grits

I promise that what follows was intended to be included in this book all along, and that it is not here as a result of the election of Jimmy Carter as president. I am a Southerner, although for the moment I live outside the South, and I retain my fondness for Southern foods. I hope and pray, for instance, that the processors of freeze-dried vegetables will someday understand that it is not enough to offer the backpacker a bland assortment of dried peas and green beans, with an occasional carrot or beet. The backpacking world would be a much better place if such delicacies as freeze-dried okra, collards, and butterbeans were widely available.

Grits are not the product of grit trees. They are the broken grains that are left when the hull and germ are removed from corn. For millions of Americans, grits are a fine way to start the day, or even end it or break it in the middle. Grits are not the most healthy food in the world, being high in calories and low in practically everything else. But they are easily available to the backpacker, and they are easy to prepare.

"Quick" grits may be bought in grocery stores and prepared according to package instructions, which usually call for adding a small quantity of grits to a pot of boiling water, to which a dash of salt has been added. You return to the boil, then reduce the heat, and cook a few minutes.

The Quaker Oats people, who seem to sell a lot of the nation's grits, have introduced Instant White Hominy Grits, which come in small envelopes simi-

lar to those used for instant oatmeal. The backpacker can transfer the contents of one of these
envelopes to a boilable plastic bag, seal it, and take
it into the field, where boiling water is added to the
mixture.

One reason Northerners don't like grits is that
Southerners forget to explain that you usually add
things to them: margarine or butter, salt and pepper,
gravy (especially red-eye ham gravy). Or you can
eat grits as you would a cereal, with milk and sugar
or honey. *Some* people even eat grits later in the day;
this will be discussed under "Lunches."

Eggs

Eggs, of course, are the traditional breakfast for
even more people than those who eat grits. But eggs
would seem to be almost out of the question for the
backpacker; they contain a lot of water and they
are somewhat prone to breakage.

It is possible, though, to include eggs in your
wilderness menu if you use a dried egg mix. These
are not available everywhere, but I have found them
frequently enough. And if you really like eggs for
breakfast, they're worth the search.

Durkee Famous Foods makes two sorts of egg
mixes: Durkee Scrambled Egg Mix and Durkee
Western Omelet Mix Deliciously Seasoned with
Onion and Green Pepper. The first comes in a foil
envelope that weighs less than an ounce, the second
in a similar package that weighs a tad over an
ounce. Each claims to be the equivalent of two
medium-sized eggs, and each contains dry milk and
other additives, in addition to the dried whole eggs.

To reconstitute the Durkee eggs, put the contents
of a package in a bowl, pot, or plastic bag, add ⅓
cup water, and mix. And *really* mix; it takes a lot

of beating, whipping, and stirring to get all the lumps out. To cook, you fry the eggs in a pan with margarine, just as you would at home.

At first, I was very skeptical of this product. I had been, you may recall, an army cook, and I had had my troubles with dehydrated eggs (which always seemed to give themselves away by turning up with a greenish tint as we set them before the hungry troops). These eggs are the proper shade of yellow and taste quite good, however, especially on a cold morning. (The same cold morning will make it twice as hard to mix the eggs and the water. If you can heat the water a little first, that helps.) Half a bacon bar, crumbled into a pan of scrambled eggs, is delicious.

Tillie Lewis Foods, Inc., produces a similar scrambled-egg packet, under the brand Eggstra, for the diet market. An envelope of Eggstra weighs less than one of Durkee's, but it claims to equal two *large* eggs.

Pancakes

Another product that may be used by backpackers more or less straight from the supermarket shelves is the "complete" pancake mix. Before such a mix was developed, the hiker who liked pancakes had to carry along eggs in some form to add to the other ingredients—usually a mixture of flour, salt, sugar, baking powder, shortening, and milk.

Now everything is available in one box, ready to be recombined with water into a pancake batter that is not markedly different from the old-fashioned one —or at least the old-fashioned store-bought one. The backpacker measures out the mix into a plastic bag at home, then adds water in the woods, mixes, and fries as usual.

One brand that has worked well for me is Aunt Jemima Complete Pancake & Waffle Mix, made by Quaker Oats. If you're the sort of person who would rather deal with smaller portions of the mix than are available in the large supermarket boxes, you might want to try the Washington brand mix. They sell a regular pancake mix, as well as a buttermilk pancake mix, in 7-ounce boxes. Inside the boxes are sealed envelopes that you can just take with you into the woods, where you combine the contents with a cup of water.

To cook pancakes in the woods, you will need something that can be called a frying pan—the top of a Sigg pot, or the frying pan–saucepan portion of the Campways cookset, or something similar. You'll also need a utensil with which to turn the cakes. The all-purpose spoon-utensil simply will not do the job; nor will the folding knife.

I solved the problem for myself by finding, in the housewares section of a department store, a flat, hard-plastic spatula. It was designed for use in a regular kitchen, so of course it was far too large for my traveling cupboard. I cut it down at both ends with a hacksaw, and it fits nicely inside my cooking pots. I would tell you the brand name of the spatula except that I cut it off.

Pancakes are hardly pancakes, of course, without some sort of syrup. Honey works nicely. Rich-Moor sells a prepared backpackers' Artificially Flavored Maple Syrup Mix that combines with boiling water and is rather heavy. Or you can make your own.

NONMAPLE SYRUP

½ cup brown sugar
squirt of oil or margarine
water

At home: Package the sugar in a plastic bag.

In the field: Put the sugar and oil or margarine into a pot, along with 2 tablespoons water. Heat over moderate flame, stirring constantly. Add a couple more tablespoons water if necessary to bring the mixture to the proper consistency. When it is producing bubbles, it is more than likely ready.

Breakfast Bars

There are also various brands of breakfast bars that the marketing geniuses are aiming at those people who are always in too much of a hurry for breakfast. Frankly, the idea of eating a thing that looks like a candy bar and calling it breakfast is revolting to me. But, of course, some people feel that way about grits.

LUNCH AND SNACKS

It may not be practical or even decent to lump together "lunch" and "snacks" in your everyday eating life, but in backpacking the situation is different.

When you're walking, skiing, or canoeing, lunch tends to be more of a break than a full-fledged meal —a time to stop and get the pack off your shoulders or the paddle out of your hands, to lean back against a tree or a boulder and take it easy for a little while, maybe even to doze for a few minutes. Food is almost secondary.

You don't want too much of it, or you'll become lazy and unable to do the afternoon's stint. Too little of it will allow you to become tired before your time, and that, too, will affect the rest of the day.

I have found, as have many backpackers I've talked with, that the best procedure is to have several snacks during the day—one during the morning and one during the afternoon, and another one at the middle of the day, which you call "lunch." If the stove is to be used, as it will be with soup, you'll want to use it at midday. The other breaks should be for foods that require no, or virtually no, preparation time and cleanup.

Peanut Butter

All of which leads us to the champion of all back-packing foods, the wonderful old standby, the food that provides satisfaction, calories, protein, and just about everything else: peanut butter.

It is compact. It stores and travels easily and requires no refrigeration. You can buy it in any grocery store in the country. When you have eaten it all, the jar it came in makes an excellent storage container and an unsurpassed bottle for shaking up homemade salad dressings. Some of the jars have cups and ounces marked on their sides. Very few people don't like the taste of peanut butter; its flavor has been imprinted on our minds and taste buds, and imprinted in a favorable way, since we were tiny children.

And it is full of good things, according to the U.S. Department of Agriculture's Handbook No. 8, *Composition of Foods*.

One hundred grams (a little more than $3\frac{1}{2}$ ounces) of a peanut butter that has small amounts of added fat, sweetener, and salt contains only 1.7 percent water; it has 582 calories, 25.5 grams of protein, 49.5 grams of fat, and 19.5 grams of carbohydrate.

By contrast, 100 grams of enriched egg noodles contains 70.4 percent water when cooked, 9.8 percent uncooked. The cooked product contains 125 calories, 4.1 grams of protein, 1.5 grams of fat, and 23.3 grams of carbohydrate. Or consider 100 grams of macaroni and cheese: 58.2 percent water, 215 calories, 8.4 grams of protein, 11.1 grams of fat, and 20.1 grams of carbohydrate.

Peanut butter even looks good next to brook trout, 100 grams of which (uncooked) contains 77.7 percent water, 101 calories, 19.2 grams of protein, 2.1 grams of fat, and no carbohydrates. (But who would stop eating after 100 grams of freshly caught brook trout?)

Peanut butter may be carried in any of a number of ways; the freezer containers and plastic Gerry Tubes mentioned earlier are two of them. The stuff also may be *eaten* in a variety of ways: on crackers or dense bread, licked off the fingers, or squirted straight from a Gerry Tube into the mouth (if you can rid your imagination of the fear that you might be eating toothpaste).

The popularity of peanut butter in its own, original form has led to the development of a number of supermarket items that incorporate the food. Some of them sound and look as if they would do a good job of filling the backpacker's need for a compact, chewy peanut-butter snack. I would like to warn you about one of them.

It's called New! Peanut Butter Crunchola with Cinnamon Raisins. The label discloses that there really is no such thing as "cinnamon raisins," but rather that cinnamon and raisins are among the numerous ingredients (there are more corn sweeteners and sugar than peanut butter, by the way).

If you compare New! etc. with the Department of Agriculture's statistics on regular old peanut butter, you see that the product is lower in calories, protein, and fat, and higher only in carbohydrates. The packaging is a prime example of wasted space and cardboard; I calculated that if the manufacturer wanted to, he or she could pack eighteen of the bars inside a box that actually contains eight. And it tastes, to me, like some kind of petroleum product. You might want to consider investing in an old-fashioned jar of peanut butter.

Or, you could invest in said jar and make your own little cylinders of peanut-butter wonderment for eating on the trail. There are lots of versions of this; I call mine

ROSE'S PEANUT BUTTER DELIGHT

½ cup pitted dates
⅓ cup cashews
½ cup raisins
¼ cup dried apples (or prunes, peaches, pears, or apricots)
¼ cup shredded coconut
¼ cup wheat germ
½ cup instant dry milk
¼ cup brown sugar
½ cup All-Bran or similar dry cereal
1½ cups peanut butter
1 cup honey

At home: Chop, as fine as possible, all the ingredients that can be chopped. Put all ingredients except peanut butter and honey through a food grinder at least twice, or until the mixture is somewhat uniform. Then mix in the peanut butter and honey. Use your hands; it's going to be a big mess anyway. Add more peanut butter or honey or both in order to achieve a texture that pleases you.

Place mixture in a bowl, cover, and refrigerate a

few hours (in order to harden it a bit). Break into small balls and roll and pat into sausage shapes or logs. Dust with a little more brown sugar, place on ungreased cookie sheet, and bake in 250° oven for 30 minutes.

When the logs have cooled, wrap each one in plastic film. Store in refrigerator until ready to use.

NOTE: This recipe bears the first name of Rose Virgona, the grande dame who presides over the fortunes of Romeo's Food Store, the fount of knowledge, pasta, and homemade Italian sausages in my part of Brooklyn. Rose knows a lot about cooking, and when she saw me buying the ingredients for this concoction she quickly guessed what I was trying to do. When I said I planned not to bake the product, but just wrap it and eat it, she grew agitated. She insisted that I bake a batch and see the difference. She was, of course, right.

Just about all the ingredients in the recipe, and the quantities of those ingredients, are highly negotiable. Only peanut butter and honey are what you might call absolutely necessary.

Gorp

Another backpacking standard, and one in which the ingredients are largely left up to the individual's discretion and imagination, is gorp, the wonderful high-energy (meaning high-calorie) mixture that tastes so good when you have just finished climbing a thousand feet practically straight up and you reward yourself with a break beside an ice-cold spring.

My first exposure to gorp came several years ago in the northern Catskills of New York State. It was wintertime, and my daughter and I, who were then relatively new to backpacking, were camping on the snow along a beautiful, and even now unspoiled, trail. We ran into a young man who was staying down the way. He was spending the seventeen days of his winter break from college in a tent made of a plastic dry-cleaning bag. He had a stove, but he hardly ever used it.

He was living almost exclusively off a gorp mixture that he had stirred, back at home, into a huge potful of milk chocolate. When the chocolate hardened, he had wrapped chunks of it in plastic, and every once in a while he broke off a piece and ate it. When he grinned, you saw that all his teeth were temporarily browned out. But he certainly had a lot of energy.

It is somewhat more healthful, especially in the wintertime, to augment your gorp with some other foods, but that's no reason to leave out gorp. Just for starters, here are some of the items that might go into your mixture. Anyone who cites specific quantities is being overfastidious and probably shouldn't be a backpacker:

Cashews, peanuts, raisins, sunflower seeds, chopped dates, apricots, currants, apples, figs, pumpkin seeds, semi-sweet chocolate bits, shredded coconut, walnuts, pecans, and wheat germ. And the item that, for me and many others, makes it authentic gorp: M&M candy bits, with or without peanut centers.

You may be tempted to add toasted sesame seeds. I have found that they just cling to everything else and don't add much flavor at all.

Soup

Soup is quite a legitimate dish for lunch. It is especially welcome in the coolness of spring and fall, and may be necessary in winter, when the mere act of stopping for the lunch break can rob you of much of your body heat.

The stores are full of soup mixes, both instant and those that cook in a few minutes. My own favorite is pea soup. It seems to be more filling and psychologically comforting than the others, but perhaps that's just a personal idiosyncrasy. Pea soup does lend itself, however, to consumption with the aforementioned peanut butter, and it's quite easy to dump some Vienna sausage or freeze-dried ham into the pot with it. With just a little extra effort, you can become elaborate.

AUGMENTED SOUP I

1 5-ounce can Vienna sausages
2 cups water
1 envelope green-pea soup mix (not instant soup; Lipton makes both kinds)
2 tablespoons dried celery flakes
1 tablespoon dried onion flakes
2 tablespoons dried cheese (American or Parmesan)

At home: Package the celery and onion flakes in a small packet of plastic film; do the same with the dried cheese. Leave the soup mix and sausage in their original packaging.

In the field: Slice the Vienna sausages and lightly brown them in the pot as it heats up, moving them constantly to avoid burning. Add the water and then the soup mix, stirring until smooth. Add celery and onion flakes. Simmer, covered, for about 10 minutes, stirring occasionally. Before eating, stir in the cheese.

NOTE: You can substitute freeze-dried ham for the Vienna sausage.

AUGMENTED SOUP II

1 envelope vegetable-beef soup mix (not instant)
¼ cup (or more or less) quick rice*
1½ cups water
⅛ to ¼ cup or more soy nuts

At home: Package the rice and soy nuts separately and leave the soup mix in its foil bag.

In the field: Put everything except the soy nuts into pot and bring to a boil. Reduce heat and cook, stirring, until rice is done (about 5 to 8 minutes). Add soy nuts at the last minute or as you eat the soup.

NOTE: If you put the soy nuts in earlier, they will quickly become soggy. Variations: Add a 5-ounce can of boned turkey or chicken or half a meat bar.

* The assumption here, as explained earlier, is that you're using Uncle Ben's Quick Rice. The proportions are not critical in this particular recipe, but in others the amount of water used is related to the brand of rice.

Grits

And then there are grits again. I swear that some people actually eat grits this way:

CHEESE-GARLIC GRITS

1 serving of grits
2 to 3 tablespoons dried cheese
1 or 2 dashes of dehydrated garlic powder

In the field: Cook the grits, either instant or quick, in the usual way. Then stir in the cheese and garlic and eat. Not as bad as it sounds.

Cheese

Cheese by itself, of course, is fine for snacks or lunch or as a supplement to soup. The best ones for the backpacker are the hard cheeses (such as American, cheddar, Edam, provolone, and Swiss) and some of the semihard ones (Monterey Jack). Stay away from the soft cheeses (Camembert, farmer cheese), which are quite perishable. Processed cheeses, which are mixtures of cheese, emulsifiers, and sometimes large quantities of water, have admirable keeping qualities but taste like junk.

Store-Bought Snacks

There are quite a few store-bought items that work well as snacks. My favorites include Nature Valley Granola Bars, which are made of rolled oats, brown sugar, coconut oil, honey, salt, sesame seeds, soy lecithin, and "natural flavoring"; and Claxton Fruit Cake, made by Claxton Bakeries, of Claxton, Georgia. The latter is an individually wrapped 1-pound cake (they come three to a box) that is almost as full of calories as a box of condensed mincemeat, and a lot better-tasting. The Claxton people will mail their cakes to you, or you can buy them at practically any cloverleaf on Interstate 95 in Georgia.

Dessert

If you're an incurable dessert person, you can take along some

INSTANT PUDDING

one-quarter of a 4½-ounce box of instant pudding,
  any flavor
2 tablespoons instant dry milk
½ cup water

At home: Remove the pudding from its box and
separate into four piles by weight. This makes enough
for four servings. (The brand I use is My-T-Fine.)
Repackage each pile into a plastic bag with 2 tablespoons dry milk. Seal bags to prevent spoilage and
leakage.

In the field: Open a bag, pour in ½ cup water,
mix well, and wait (5 minutes or more) until it sets
into a pudding-like mass. One store-bought box
makes 4 servings.

NOTE: In cold weather, the stuff will taste more
like pudding, but refrigeration is not required. Don't
be fooled by the initial thinness of the mixture; it
will eventually thicken. No cleanup required if you
eat out of the bag. This pudding is extremely sweet
(the chief ingredient is sugar) but makes a passable
dessert for one of those inevitable days when you're
tired and hungry and have convinced yourself that
you really need some dessert.

6

DINNER

Now comes the evening meal, the one that's supposed to be the payoff for the long, hard, exhausting, but also exhilarating day of walking, exploring, paddling, climbing, or sitting and meditating on mountains.

As mentioned more than once before, one component of the evening meals in what I call my system is starch—most often in the form of potatoes, pasta, or rice. Each of these can be cooked easily and relatively quickly, utilizing a minimum of water, time, and fuel. In virtually all cases, since your cooking will be of the one-pot variety, you'll be preparing the starches in concert with your other ingredients, all at once.

Just the same, here are the basic rules for preparing the basic starches separately. Each makes one hefty serving (as do all the recipes, unless otherwise noted):

BASIC MASHED POTATOES

squirt of oil or margarine
1¼ cup water
1 cup instant mashed potatoes
dash salt
4 tablespoons instant dry milk

At home: Package together the potatoes, salt, and dry milk.

In the field: Add squirt of oil to water and bring to a boil. Stir in the potato-salt-milk package and remove from the heat. Stir well and wait about one minute before eating.

BASIC NOODLES OR PASTA

dash of salt
2 cups water
1 cup noodles or pasta (see note)

At home: Package the pasta in a plastic bag.

In the field: Bring salted water to a boil, dump in the pasta, stir a moment, and boil until done.

NOTE: The amount of pasta that constitutes, for you, "one serving" may vary considerably. One cup of Creamettes macaroni makes an abundance of pasta; a cup of egg noodles might not. You'll have to experiment to see what works best for you. The amount of water varies, as well. You *could* use what the manufacturer suggests on the back of the box, but that's likely to be a lot of water. The backpacker usually wants to use as little as possible. Creamettes will take 2 cups; some thin spaghetti will require more. I don't find that the reduction in liquid makes a tremendous difference in the quality of the finished product, especially if you stir the pasta occasionally to keep it from collecting on the bottom of the pot and sticking there.

Ordinarily you will want to drain the pasta after it's cooked. At home you'd do this with a colander or strainer, but in the woods you'll have to let the water drain out as you tilt the pot while opening its lid a fraction of an inch. This can be disastrous if you're not careful. I once left half a pound of spaghetti on the ground for the woods creatures because I relaxed my grip on the lid while draining. Just don't try to hurry up the process and you'll be okay.

BASIC RICE

¾ cup Uncle Ben's Quick Rice (see note)
squirt of oil or margarine (optional)
dash salt
½ cup water

At home: Package the rice and salt together.

In the field: Put everything into the pot, bring to a vigorous boil, cover, and simmer until the rice is ready—until it has absorbed the water and tastes more or less like rice. This takes from 6 to 9 minutes.

NOTE: If you want to use Minute Rice, the manufacturer will tell you to use equal portions of rice and water, a little salt, and optional oil. You bring the water, salt, and oil to a boil, stir in the rice, cover, remove from heat, and let stand for 5 or more minutes.

As noted before, many of the meats and other protein sources cited in these recipes may be considered interchangeable—up to a point, at least (you probably wouldn't want to substitute canned turkey for beef in a spaghetti dish, or maybe you would). To make things even more interchangeable, here are two recipes for producing your own preserved beef at home.

HOMEMADE DEHYDRATED BEEF

1 pound (or more or less) ground beef

At home: Brown the ground beef in a skillet, breaking it into small bits with a utensil. Drain fat, if any, and let beef stand for a few minutes. Then turn it out onto a couple of thicknesses of paper towels. Cover with more towels and pat the beef to dry it.

Spread the beef on a cookie sheet or aluminum foil and put in a 150°F oven—close to the lowest setting—for 8 hours or so. (The point is not to cook the meat in the oven but rather to drive the moisture from it.) Store the end product in a plastic bag in the refrigerator until ready for use. One pound of fresh meat makes about ¾ cup of finished product.

In the field: Sprinkle the dried beef into soups, stews, and other dishes as you would any other meat.

NOTE: Use sparingly. Remember that the handful of tiny beef-like specks you end up with started out as a pound of ground beef. And use it early-on during hot-weather expeditions. The meat keeps well, in my experience, but there's no sense in taking chances.

The next recipe is just one of many ways to prepare your own jerky. To jerk meat, as our ancestors did with great regularity, means to cut it into strips and to dry it, usually in the sun. Not only is the meat preserved in this way, but it also is dehydrated, making it lighter—two circumstances which should be attractive to the backpacker. Often the meat is subjected, before drying, to soaking in a marinade to tenderize it and give it some flavor.

HOMEMADE JERKY

Marinade:
½ cup red wine
¼ cup soy sauce
2 tablespoons Worcestershire sauce
½ tablespoon monosodium glutamate
1 clove garlic, minced (or dash garlic powder)
⅛ tablespoon black pepper
1 small onion, sliced

Meat:

Portion (1 or more pounds) of flank steak

At home: Cut the steak into thin strips, along the grain. Discard the fat. Soak the meat in marinade overnight, at room temperature, in a covered bowl. Next day, arrange the strips of meat on the wire rack of an oven, with a pan or foil beneath them to catch any drippings. Turn oven to 150°F and dry the meat for 10 to 12 hours. Bag, seal, and refrigerate the jerky until needed.

In the field: Use as you would any meat, or eat the jerky as is for a snack.

NOTE: You may want to experiment with the marinade, to bring in tastes that particularly appeal to you. Try adding the following to the foregoing marinade: 2 bay leaves, 3 whole cloves, 1 tablespoon wine vinegar, dashes of thyme and oregano. Or you may want to make the marinade much simpler, so that the taste of the meat is altered as little as possible. In warm weather, treat this as you would the Homemade Dehydrated Beef.

The following item is not, itself, a dinner, but it makes a fine side dish, or it may be eaten with a pot of soup as a complete meal. For a store-bought version of this dish, see the section titled "Exotica."

POTATO PANCAKES

¼ cup instant mashed potatoes
1 tablespoon dried minced onions
1 tablespoon dried soup greens (or a mixture of whatever dehydrated vegetables you might have around)
dash salt
2–6 tablespoons water
oil or margarine

At home: Package everything together but the water and oil.

In the field: Add enough water to the potato-vegetable mixture to make a smooth dough. As little as 2 tablespoonfuls may do it. Mix well. Form into thin patties or pones with your hands. Fry over moderate heat in the oil or margarine, turning once. Makes about three fair-sized pancakes.

NOTE: Resist the temptation to turn the cakes over until they're ready; otherwise you run the risk of having them disintegrate into a lot of very little, ir-regularly-shaped pancakes.

Now come the main meals, starting with those that use pasta and noodles as their starch base.

MACARONI AND JERKY

½ cup Homemade Jerky (page 91)
2 cups water
dash salt
1 cup macaroni (see note)
1 tablespoon dried onions
2 envelopes instant cream of mushroom soup mix
margarine (optional)

At home: Package the macaroni and onions to-gether, the meat separately; leave the soup mix in its envelopes.

In the field: Soak jerky in the water for 15 minutes. Remove from water, drain, and set aside. Bring water, with salt, to a boil. Add macaroni, meat, and onions and boil until pasta is almost done, stirring frequently to avoid sticking. Add soup mix and mar-garine (optional).

NOTE: This recipe is based on the use of the Creamettes brand of macaroni. You may find that other brands and other sorts of pasta will require less or more water. If more water is used, you will need to drain some of it after the pasta is cooked, in order to reconstitute the cream of mushroom to the proper consistency.

TOMATO, MACARONI AND BEEF

2 cups water
dash salt
3 tablespoons dried onions
2 tablespoons dried bell peppers
2 packages instant tomato soup mix
1 cup macaroni
½ meat bar

At home: Package separately: pasta; onions and peppers. Leave soup mix in its envelopes.

In the field: Put water, with salt, in the pot and start heating. Add onions and peppers and bring to boil. Add soup mix and macaroni. Boil, stirring frequently, until macaroni is almost done. Add meat and continue cooking until pasta is done and meat is heated through.

NOTE: Other sorts of meat may be substituted, and instant vegetable soup mix may replace the tomato soup mix.

BASIC SPAGHETTI I

spice packet: dried onions, oregano, garlic, basil, and bay leaf
oil or margarine
dash salt
2½ cups water
1 cup spaghetti (or about ¼ pound)
1 8-ounce can tomato sauce

At home: For the spice packet, roll the spices in a small square of plastic film and drop the packet in the plastic bag in which the spaghetti is packed.

In the field: Add spice packet and squirt of oil to salted water and bring to boil. Add spaghetti; boil until almost done. Pour out all but about 1 cup of water, retaining as many of the spices as possible. Add tomato sauce and continue cooking about 5 minutes, until pasta is done.

NOTE: A variety of meats—beef, jerky, tuna, Vienna sausage, even chicken—may be mixed in with this concoction at the same time the tomato sauce is added. This meal is heavier than most because of the weight of the tomato sauce. Spaghettis II, III, and IV are somewhat lighter. It's also worth pointing out that spaghetti of the long, thin sort is hard to eat with just a spoon. But you'll be in the woods and nobody will be watching.

BASIC SPAGHETTI II

Follow recipe for Basic Spaghetti I, but substitute 1 6-ounce can of tomato paste for the heavier can of tomato sauce.

BASIC SPAGHETTI III

2½ cups water
oil or margarine
dash salt
1 cup spaghetti
2 envelopes instant tomato soup mix
1 envelope store-bought spaghetti sauce mix (see note)

At home: Package the pasta by itself; leave the other ingredients in their original containers.

In the field: Bring water, with squirt of oil and dash of salt, to a boil. Add pasta. Cook, stirring, until almost done. Pour out some water, leaving about 1½ cups. Add soup and sauce mixes, stirring in well to break up lumps. Simmer about 5 minutes or until the pasta is done and the sauce well mixed, stirring occasionally to keep it from sticking to the pot.

NOTE: The spaghetti sauce mixes are widely available in supermarkets, where they come in small foil envelopes. The brand I use, Spatini, is made of dehydrated onion, garlic, and carrots, along with other things. It is not perfect, but it'll do in the woods. You may want to augment the store-bought sauce mix with onions or garlic if you go heavy on those ingredients at home.

BASIC SPAGHETTI SAUCE IV

Follow recipe for Sauce III, but substitute 2 envelopes of instant vegetable soup for the envelope of store-bought sauce mix. Also throw in a spice packet of dried onions, oregano, garlic, basil, and bay leaf.

SPAGHETTI WITH CLAM SAUCE

dash salt
2½ cups water
1 cup thin spaghetti
spice packet: dehydrated parsley, garlic, oregano
1 6½-ounce can minced clams

At home: Wrap the spices in plastic film and drop the packet into a bag with the spaghetti and seal.

In the field: Bring salted water to a boil; add pasta and cook until almost done. Carefully drain off as much water as possible. Add contents of spice packet and clams (including their broth) and simmer 5 minutes or so, until the clams are thoroughly heated but not so long that they become tough.

NOTE: This dish is prepared almost exactly as it would be in a comfortable kitchen at home. All that's lacking is the garlic bread that ought to accompany it.

VIENNA SAUSAGE AND PASTA I

2¼ cups water
1 cup macaroni
1 envelope vegetable-beef soup mix (not instant)
1 5-ounce can Vienna sausage

At home: Package the pasta, leaving soup mix and sausages in original containers.

In the field: Bring water to a boil and add pasta. Boil, stirring occasionally, for all but the last 5 minutes of the time required to cook the pasta. Add soup mix and sausages and return to boil, stirring frequently. Lower heat and cook until pasta is done.

NOTE: When you experiment with this dish, leave salt out of the boiling water until you are satisfied with the final product; the soup mix (the brand I use is Lipton's) is quite salty. For variations, add soy sauce, Parmesan or dried American cheese, or dried chives.

VIENNA SAUSAGE AND PASTA II

dash salt
2 cups water
1 cup macaroni
2 envelopes instant cream of mushroom soup mix
1 5-ounce can Vienna sausage
margarine (optional)

At home: Package the pasta, leaving soup and sausages in original containers.

In the field: Bring salted water to boil. Add pasta and cook until done; most of the water should be absorbed. Add soup mix and sausages and mix quickly and thoroughly. Add margarine (optional).

NOTE: This is a basic, quick meal. You can substitute a variety of other meats for the Vienna sausages: tuna, chicken, turkey, beef, ham, sliced salami, and others.

UNCREAMED MACARONI WITH CHEESE

dash salt
2 cups water
1 cup macaroni
1 tablespoon instant dry milk
4 tablespoons dried American cheese food
margarine (optional)

At home: Package together the dry milk and cheese food. Package the macaroni separately.

In the field: Bring salted water to boil. Add pasta and cook until done. Drain off most of the water, add milk and dry cheese food (and optional margarine) over low heat, and stir in.

NOTE: To make this a more nutritious meal, add a small can of tuna or Vienna sausage or other meat at the time you add the milk and cheese. Be careful, toward the end, about letting the cheese burn to the bottom of the pan.

CREAMED MACARONI WITH CHEESE

dash salt
2 cups water
1 packet or cube of chicken bouillon
1 cup macaroni
2 envelopes instant cream of mushroom soup mix
4 tablespoons dried American cheese food
1 tablespoon instant dry milk

At home: Package the cheese food and dry milk together in plastic film and put the packet inside a bag that contains the loose macaroni, the bouillon in its wrapping, and the envelopes of soup mix.

In the field: Bring salted water to boil. Add bouillon and macaroni and cook until the macaroni is almost done. Drain a little of the liquid, leaving about 1¼ cup. Add soup mix and stir vigorously. Sprinkle cheese-milk mixture over the macaroni. Simmer a few minutes, stirring frequently.

NOTE: This can be eaten as a vegetarian dish or as the basis for a meat dish. Tuna tastes especially good here. Add it to the mixture at the time you put in the soup mix.

MACARONI AND MEAT IN TOMATO SAUCE

dash salt
2 cups water
1 cup macaroni
1 tablespoon dried onions
1 tablespoon dried bell peppers
about ⅓ cup Homemade Dehydrated Beef (see page 90)
2 envelopes instant tomato soup mix
margarine (optional)

At home: Make a plastic-film packet of the onions and bell peppers; put it and the soup mix and separately packaged meat into a plastic bag containing the loose macaroni.

In the field: Bring salted water to a boil; add and cook the macaroni. About halfway through, add the onions and peppers. When macaroni is almost done, drain some water, leaving about 1¼ cups. Add meat and tomato soup mix, stirring everything in well. Simmer until meat is heated through and the pasta is done. Stir in margarine (optional).

There are two meals that come more or less straight from the store. The first is an old standby of long-distance hikers; the second is less well known but, I think, quite superior.

KRAFT NOODLE AND CHEESE DINNER

The dinner, which weighs 6¼ ounces, comes in a box. It calls for 6 cups of boiling water; you can get away with 3. The manufacturer also specifies ¼ cup milk; substitute 3 tablespoons instant dry milk and a little of the leftover water that was used for boiling. The noodles in the Kraft dinner are loose inside the box, and should be repackaged in something lighter. The "cheese" mixture comes in a foil envelope. This is one of several packaged "dinners" from Kraft.

PENNSYLVANIA DUTCH MACARONI AND CHEESE

This one comes in a foil envelope, and there is no need to repackage. The instructions call for only 2¼ cups of water for boiling, and the claim that the product cooks in 7 minutes is correct. One package, which has a net weight of 5 ounces, produces enough food for two people if the macaroni is augmented with some sort of meat.

This is one of the best, and most honest, such products I have found since I began my search for supermarket foods that are compatible with backpacking. The manufacturer is Pennsylvania Dutch-Megs, Inc. The firm also sells similarly packaged, and similarly good, products that use noodles as their starch base: noodles and butter sauce, beef sauce, cheese sauce, and chicken sauce.

Following are some recipes that employ instant mashed potatoes. This is a more difficult starch to work with, I think, than noodles, pasta, and rice. I have had to resort to a two-pot method to produce anything other than a soggy mess. By all means experiment with it at home in one pot; you may be more successful. The flavor and texture of mashed potatoes are welcome on the trail. They do not have the "freeze-dried taste," and they are lightweight and easy to carry and prepare.

MASHED POTATOES, CHICKEN, AND GRAVY

(two pots)
1 5-ounce can boned chicken or turkey
water
1 serving gravy (see below)
Basic Mashed Potatoes (page 88)

At home: Package potatoes and gravy separately; keep meat in can.

In the field: Open the lid on the can of chicken and squeeze whatever liquid is inside into a pot (which may be quite small). Add water to make about 4 ounces. Add home-packaged packet of instant gravy (see note below). Stir gravy powder in well and bring to boil. Add chicken. Simmer the mixture about 1 minute.

More or less simultaneously, fix a serving of mashed potatoes in another pot. When everything is done, pour the gravy-chicken mixture over the potatoes.

To package gravy: Purchase an envelope of store-bought gravy mix, preferably one that is supposed to cook quickly. *At home:* Break open the envelope and separate contents into two piles, by weight or by eye. Reseal the two portions in boilable bags. Each portion will make about ½ cup gravy.

To make gravy separately in the field: Most gravy

manufacturers call for putting water into pot, adding mix, bringing to a boil, and simmering a short period. Some gravies are marketed as being especially for chicken or turkey; others just call themselves "brown gravy."

CHICKEN AND MASHED POTATOES IN WHITE WINE SAUCE

(two pots)
Basic Mashed Potatoes (page 88)
¾ cup water
1 5-ounce can boned chicken or turkey
4 tablespoons instant dry milk
1 envelope white wine sauce mix (see note)

At home: Put wine sauce mix and dry milk together in plastic bag; package potatoes separately; leave meat in can.

In the field: Prepare mashed potatoes in one pot. In another pot, combine water, liquid from can of chicken, and contents of milk-wine sauce packet. Bring to boil. Add chicken. Simmer uncovered 3 to 5 minutes, or until mixture tastes right.

NOTE: The white wine sauce mix I have used, which tastes nowhere like the real item, is made by Lawry's Foods.

CREAMED CHICKEN

(two pots)
2 dried Chinese mushrooms (optional; see note)
¾ cup water
Basic Mashed Potatoes (page 88)
2 envelopes instant cream of chicken flavor soup mix
1 5-ounce can boned chicken or turkey

At home: Leave soup mix in its envelopes and meat in its can. Package mushrooms and potatoes separately.

In the field: If using mushrooms, soak them in the water for about 20 minutes, remove, and slice into half-thumbnail-sized pieces. Prepare mashed potatoes in one pot. In another, bring the water to a boil, reduce heat, and add soup mix, chicken, and mushrooms. Simmer until everything is heated through.

NOTE: The Chinese mushrooms are not essential, but they add a delightful flavor to the dish. For information on obtaining them, see the section titled "Exotica." This dish is every bit as good when made with rice or noodles instead of potatoes. For rice, it becomes a one-pot meal: Just use ¾ cup rice and a little more water. It's also good when served over bannock (page 114–15).

Rice-based dishes are quite popular with backpackers, myself included, because the quick-cooking rice is compact (although not as compact as regular rice), it blends well with other ingredients, and it requires very little water for cooking.

MORE OR LESS VIENNESE VIENNA SAUSAGE

1¼ cup water
¾ cup quick rice
1 tablespoon dried onions
½ tablespoon dried celery flakes
dash salt
2 envelopes instant cream of mushroom soup mix
⅛ tablespoon dried mustard
⅛ tablespoon dried dill weed
1 5-ounce can Vienna sausage

At home: Wrap the dry mustard and dill together in a piece of plastic film and place it inside a plastic bag that contains the rice, onions, and celery. Seal the bag. The Vienna sausage travels in its own can, of course, and the soup mix stays in its envelopes.

In the field: Stir together in a pot the water, rice, onions, celery, dash salt, and envelopes of soup mix. Bring to a boil. Turn heat down to simmer and add mustard, dill, and sausages (which may be sliced). Cover and simmer until rice is done (about 5 minutes).

SAVANNAH RED RICE

1 cup water
1 tablespoon dried onions
1 tablespoon dried bell peppers
1 envelope instant tomato soup mix
¾ cup quick rice
½ or more bacon bar

At home: Wrap the onions and peppers together in plastic film. Package everything else separately.

In the field: Put the water, onions, and peppers in a pot and bring to a boil. Add soup mix and rice and return to boil. Turn down to simmer and cook until rice is done. While waiting for the rice, crumble the bacon bar into small chunks (it may crumble by itself as you unwrap it). When rice is ready, stir the bacon bar into mixture.

NOTE: The meat in a Wilson's bacon bar is precooked; you only have to heat it. If you don't want to bother with dried onions and bell peppers, substitute an envelope of instant vegetable soup mix for the tomato mix.

If you're ever in Savannah, find a restaurant that serves the less rapid version of this dish. It will convert you instantly into a lover of lowcountry cooking.

VIENNA SAUSAGE AND RED RICE

margarine or oil
1 5-ounce can Vienna sausage
1 tablespoon (or more or less) dried onions
¾ cup water
¾ cup quick rice
1 envelope instant tomato soup mix

At home: The soup mix stays in its envelope, the meat in its can. Package everything else separately.

In the field: Put some margarine or oil in saucepan or pot. Slice the sausages and sauté them for 1 or 2 minutes; toward the end add the onions. Add the water and rice and bring to a boil. Turn down to simmer, add soup mix, stir well, and simmer until rice is done (about 5 to 9 minutes).

NOTE: If your stove lacks a low flame, and if your pan or pot is made of thin material, be sure to keep the sausages moving as you sauté them. Otherwise they're likely to burn and stick to the bottom.

SHRIMP CREOLE, SORT OF

oil or margarine
1 tablespoon dried onions
⅛ tablespoon or more dried garlic
½ tablespoon dried bell peppers
½ tablespoon dried celery flakes
1 8-ounce can tomato sauce
Creole spice packet: dash each of cayenne pepper, basil, rosemary, thyme, filé, marjoram, savory, mace, parsley, and ½ bay leaf
½ cup water
¾ cup quick rice
1 small can shrimp

At home: Put the components of the Creole spice packet into a square of plastic film. In another square put the onions, garlic, bell peppers, and celery flakes. Place these packets inside a plastic bag containing the rice. Leave shrimps and tomato sauce in original containers.

In the field: Squirt a little oil or margarine into saucepan or pot and sauté onion, garlic, bell peppers, and celery flakes briefly. Add tomato sauce, Creole spice packet, water, and rice; bring to boil, cover, and simmer for a few minutes, until rice is done. About 2 minutes after you start it simmering, stir the shrimps into the mixture, carefully so as to avoid breaking them up.

NOTE: This is a heavy meal (in terms of the weight of the ingredients, if not the effect of the food on the stomach), and you might want to save it for special occasions. Some variations are possible: Substitute 2 envelopes of instant tomato soup mix for the much heavier can of tomato sauce. Or substitute 1 envelope of tomato-soup mix and 1 of vegetable-soup mix. Most real Creole shrimp has a ham component as well. I experimented with those brown fragments that are supposed to taste like bacon, but they're awful. You might want to throw in a package of freeze-dried ham chunks. Filé, a thickener that comes from the sassafras leaf, is often associated with the word "gumbo." You can buy it throughout Louisiana and in spice markets that take their work seriously, or remove it by hand from sassafras trees.

QUICK CHICKEN AND RICE

¾ cup quick rice
1 tablespoon dried onions
1 tablespoon dried celery flakes
1 tablespoon dried bell peppers
¾ cup water
1 5-ounce can boned chicken or turkey

At home: Package the rice, onions, celery, and peppers together.

In the field: Put everything into the pot, bring to a boil, and simmer covered for about 5 minutes, or until the rice is done.

NOTE: If you'd like the chicken to have a little more bite, and to disintegrate less in the pot, try holding it out until the last couple of minutes. For slight variation, add a touch of soy sauce to the mixture.

QUICK CREAMED TUNA, RICE, AND PEAS

1 3½-ounce can tuna, packed in oil
¾ cup quick rice
2 envelopes instant cream of mushroom soup mix
3-5 tablespoons freeze-dried peas
dash salt
1 cup water

At home: Package together the rice, salt, and peas. Tuna and soup mix stay in their containers.

In the field: Put everything together in the pot, stir well, and bring to a boil. Cover and simmer until the rice is done.

CREAMED TUNA AND CHEESE WITH RICE AND PEAS

1 cup water
1 3½-ounce can tuna
3-5 tablespoons freeze-dried peas
1 chicken bouillon cube or envelope
1 envelope instant cream of mushroom soup mix
dried American cheese food
¾ cup quick rice

At home: The tuna travels in its can, the soup mix in its envelope. Pack the peas and chicken bouillon together and the cheese and rice separately.

In the field: Put the water in the pot; squeeze into it the oil that comes with the tuna. Add the peas and bouillon and wait about 10 minutes. Bring mixture to a boil; stir in soup mix and cheese (2 or more tablespoonfuls, according to taste). Add rice, bring to boil, turn down to simmer, add tuna, cover, and simmer about 5 minutes, until rice is done.

VERY MOCK SHRIMP DE JONGHE

1 small can shrimp
spice packet: ⅛ tablespoon garlic, 1½ tablespoons dry parsley, and a dash each of rosemary, marjoram, and tarragon.
2 tablespoons oil or margarine
½ cup water
¾ cup quick rice
about 2 tablespoonfuls dry sherry, in Austrian bottle

At home: Make up the spice packet and tuck it inside the bag containing the rice.

In the field: Drain shrimps. Briefly sauté contents of spice packet in the oil or margarine. Add water and stir in rice. Bring to boil, then turn heat down to simmer. Gently stir in shrimps. Cover and simmer about 5 minutes, until rice is done. At last moment, stir in the sherry.

Curry is one of my all-time favorite foods. A dispute rages over whether curry powder, and the dishes that are flavored with it and called curries, are more Indian or British, but I think it's safe to say that curry is as much a national dish in India as hamburger is in the United States.

The powder comes not from a single source, but is a mixture of spices, with about as many different mixtures as there are people who mix them. Some, but by no means all, of the spices that turn up in curry powder are coriander, fenugreek, turmeric, cumin, various peppers (including cayenne), bay leaves, celery seed, cloves, ginger, cardamom, mace, and cinnamon.

You can spend a lot of time shopping around for various curry powders, or you can mix your own.

Several condiments are often served with curries, and some of them can be taken along on a back-packing trip without weighing you down too much: peanuts, cashews, shredded coconut, raisins, even a portion of chutney sauce in an Austrian bottle. Once I tried some dried banana chips, hoping that they would recall the flavor and texture of thin slices of fresh banana that sometimes come on the condiment tray in an Indian restaurant, but I think that was carrying it too far.

A fairly basic backpacker's curry sauce may be constructed by blending 1 to 3 tablespoonfuls (or more) of your favorite curry powder with two envelopes of the by-now-omnipresent instant cream of mushroom soup mix, then stirring the mixture into some boiling water. You might find—even if you're a dedicated curry lover at home—that you need less powder in the woods. I have noticed, in myself, that when I'm backpacking I often do not want, or need, my foods as spicy as at home. Perhaps it's that being out there with nature makes everything more real, and one doesn't require the extra little jolts that come from a dose of cayenne.

CHICKEN CURRY WITH NOODLES

3 cups water
1½ cup egg noodles
2 tablespoons freeze-dried peas
dash salt
1 5-ounce can boned chicken
2 envelopes instant cream of mushroom soup mix
½ tablespoon dried parsley
½ tablespoon dried celery flakes
1 or more tablespoons curry powder

At home: Pack the noodles, peas, and salt together; pack the curry powder, parsley, and celery together; keep the soup in its envelopes, the chicken in its can.

In the field: Bring water to a boil and add the noodles, peas, and salt; boil until the noodles are almost done. Carefully drain all but about 1¼ cup water. Add chicken, soup mix, parsley, celery, and curry powder. Mix well while cooking a little longer.

NOTE: Other sources of protein may be easily substituted for the chicken.

CHICKEN CURRY WITH RICE

2 envelopes instant cream of mushroom or cream
    of chicken flavor soup mix
¾ cup quick rice
1 tablespoon or more curry powder
2 tablespoons freeze-dried peas
½ tablespoon dried celery flakes
½ tablespoon dried parsley
½ tablespoon dried onions
1 cup water
1 5-ounce can boned chicken

At home: Package together the rice, curry powder, peas, celery, parsley, and onion. Leave the soup in its envelopes and the chicken in its can.

In the field: Put everything except the chicken in the pot, stir to mix well, and bring to a boil. Add chicken and simmer covered until rice is done.

NOTE: Other meats may be substituted for the chicken.

QUICK CREAMED CURRIED TUNA AND RICE

1 3½-ounce can tuna
¾ cup quick rice
1 tablespoon or more curry powder
2 envelopes instant cream of mushroom or New England chowder soup mix
1 cup water

At home: Leave tuna and soup in their containers; package rice and curry powder separately.

In the field: Put everything in the pot, mix well, bring to a boil, turn down to simmer, cover, and simmer until rice is done.

CURRY TABITHA

¾ cup quick rice
2 envelopes instant cream of mushroom soup mix
1 tablespoon or more curry powder
1 cup water
1 tablespoon to ½ cup peanuts or cashews

At home: Leave soup in envelope. Pack rice and curry powder together, nuts separately.

In the field: Put everything except the peanuts in the pot, mix well, and bring to a boil. Cover and simmer until rice is done. Stir in peanuts at last moment.

NOTE: This recipe was suggested by the intuitive cook I mentioned earlier. You can easily add parsley, freeze-dried peas, onions, and garlic to this recipe. Just put them in with everything else. Cashews taste especially good here as substitutes for the peanuts. Raisins can be added in an amount roughly equal to the amount of peanuts. Put them in when you add the nuts. Try *un*salted roasted peanuts, too.

BEEF AND VEGETABLE CURRY

1 cup water
1 package vegetable-beef soup mix (not an instant mix)
¾ cup quick rice
2 tablespoons dried chives or onions
1 tablespoon or more curry powder
½ meat bar (or other form of protein)

At home: Package the rice, curry, and chives or onions together; the rest separately.

In the field: Start the water heating in the pot; add soup mix and stir it in well. When water reaches boil, stir in rice, chives or onions, and curry powder. Reduce flame to simmer, add the meat, and simmer 5 minutes or until the rice is done.

NOTE: You may not need to add salt to this meal. The vegetable-beef soup mix (or at least the one made by Lipton) is very salty. If you're substituting peanuts or cashews for the meat, do not add them to the mixture until just before serving. Otherwise, they'll get soggy. Be sure to break up the little lumps of beef-type stuff in the soup mix when you add it to the water. If you bite into a chunk, you might not like it.

SHRIMP CURRY

1 small can shrimp
¾ cup quick rice
1 cup water
2 envelopes instant cream of mushroom soup mix
1 tablespoon or more curry powder
1 tablespoon or more raisins

At home: Leave shrimps and soup in their containers. Package everything else separately.

In the field: Drain shrimps. Add rice to the water and bring to boil. Add soup mix and curry powder, return to boil, cover, and simmer until rice is almost done. At last minute, add shrimps and raisins.

BREAD, EXOTICA, AND A FEW LOOSE ENDS

You're probably pretty tired of instant cream of mushroom soup mix by now. But if you give it a try, and lace it with enough spices, herbs, and other delicious things, it might just make your backpacking meals a little more enjoyable.

BREAD

Maybe you'll miss bread. Bread is a generally unwelcome guest in the backpacker's pack, because it takes up a lot of room and doesn't keep very well. There are a few bread-type formulations, though, that you might want to consider, especially if you really like the stuff.

One is the ancient trailpersons' standby, bannock. Bannock is a nonyeast bread that requires only a few ingredients and a rather deft hand holding the frying pan. Here are two versions.

REGULAR OLD BANNOCK

1 cup flour
⅓ tablespoon (1 teaspoon) baking powder
dash salt
oil or margarine
water

At home: Package the flour, baking powder, and salt together in a large, tough plastic bag.

In the field: Introduce a little oil or margarine into the bag, and slowly add enough water to give the mixture the consistency of dough. You're pretty much going to have to mix it with your hands. Flatten it out into a cake, and fry it in a little oil, very slowly.

NOTE: If you end up with a bread that has its outside a delicious, golden brown and its inside a somewhat uncooked, doughy mass, do not despair. Just pretend you're an ancient trailperson.

BISQUICK BANNOCK

6 to 8 tablespoons water
1 cup Bisquick buttermilk baking mix
oil or margarine

At home: Package the baking mix separately in a large, tough plastic bag.

In the field: Add the water to the mix. Use your hands. You can lick off what sticks, just as you did when you were a kid. Put some oil or margarine into a saucepan, frying pan, or Sigg lid and heat over lowest possible flame. Pat the dough into a cake about ½ inch thick. Fry it, as gently as possible, turning it often, until done.

NOTE: The trick is making the cake thin enough so the center is done, but not so thin that it turns into a pancake. You may want to practice at home. The end product is wonderful, with absolutely no freeze-dried taste. Works well with gravies, jam, margarine, honey, or as something to throw into a stew or soup. Try adding some dried dill to the mixture. Try adding some curry powder. It may help if you can cover the frying pan with something—a lid, the other half of the cookset—to help the cake cook more thoroughly without burning.

DUMPLINGS

½ cup water
1 cup Bisquick buttermilk baking mix
3 tablespoons instant dry milk

At home: Package the mix and milk together in a sturdy plastic bag.

In the field: Add the water to the mix in the plastic bag and mix well. Spoon the mixture into a stew or soup, and cook uncovered until the dumplings are done—10 minutes or longer.

ALABAMA CORNPONE

1 cup water
1 cup cornmeal (stone-ground, if possible)
½ tablespoon salt
oil or margarine

At home: Package cornmeal and salt together in a boilable plastic bag.

In the field: Bring the water to a boil. Add it to the cornmeal-salt mixture and stir well. Set the mixture aside for a few minutes. In the meantime, squirt oil into frying pan or pot lid and heat it. Using your hands, pat the cornmeal mixture into pones—flat cakes that are round and maybe ¾ inch thick. If you do it the correct Alabama way, your fingers will leave their impressions in the cake. Rhode Islanders do it more smoothly. Fry the cakes over medium heat, turning once.

NOTE: Try to overcome the temptation, here as in potato pancakes, to turn the pones before they are ready. Experimentation will lead you to the perfect moment. Experiment, too, with adding a little curry powder to the mixture. If you try this recipe at home, throw some bacon fat into the cornmeal mixture.

And five or six hours before, set some mustard greens on to cook, and . . .

You may find that you have room for a real homemade bread, in which case the following recipe is perfect. You cook it at home and take it along. The recipe is not mine; it comes from *The Deaf Smith Country Cookbook*, by Marjorie Winn Ford, Susan Hillyard, and Mary Faulk Koock (Macmillan, 1973), which is a very good and thorough book about "natural" foods. (I am disturbed only by the fact that the copyright holder is listed as Arrowhead Mills, which sells ingredients called for in the cookbook.) This is their recipe for "Phyllis's Bread," which I have found to be delightful at home and on the trail:

PHYLLIS'S BREAD

- 1 tablespoon dry yeast
- 2½ cups warm water
- 3 tablespoons unrefined corn-germ oil [I use peanut oil]
- 4 tablespoons raw honey or unsulfured molasses
- 5½ to 6 cups whole-wheat flour
- 1½ teaspoons sea salt

At home: Dissolve the yeast in the warm water; add the oil and honey. Mix the flour and salt; add the liquids. Mix well with hands, adding a little more flour if needed. Cover and let rise until double (about 1½ hours). Knead down. Shape the dough into 2 loaves. Place in oiled loaf pans. Allow to rise again until nearly doubled. Bake 10 minutes at 400°F. Reduce the heat to 350°F and bake 20 minutes more. Cool on rack. Makes two loaves, 9 by 5 inches.

EXOTICA

If you haunt the grocery stores of what have come to be called our "ethnic neighborhoods," you're likely to find a number of ingredients that fit well into the backpacker's kitchen. Most of the fun is in the finding, but here are a few suggestions from my own experience:

Couscous. A durum-wheat product that is a staple of the Middle Eastern diet. It's a delightful starch that carries and cooks easily.

Sun-dried mulberries from Turkey. They are sweet and delicious, perfect for eating during breaks. They, the couscous, and a number of other wonderful foods are available from Sahadi Importing Company, 187 Atlantic Avenue, Brooklyn, New York, 11201. Sahadi has done business by mail order, but they announced in the spring of 1977 that they were suspending the service temporarily. They will, however, ship foodstuffs to stores (not individuals) that request them. It's worth a trip to Brooklyn to see the store.

Chinese mushrooms. They are lightweight and add a lot to any dish.

Dried Chinese shrimp. Rehydrate them in water and fry them or add to other dishes. These, the mushrooms, and a number of other items are available in the Chinatowns of a dozen American cities.

Instant Chinese noodles. These may not be exotic for long; recently I saw some under the La Choy label, which means even suburbanites are eating them. They are small, lightweight packets of dehydrated noodles that you rehydrate by adding a little boiling water and waiting a few minutes. Some come with a flavor packet; all can be combined with meats. My favorite brand is Kung Fu, the flavor packet of which contains pepper oil and hits you like a brown belt. Would be fine for a cold-weather lunch.

Knorr Potato Pancake Mix. This is imported from West Germany, makes fewer pancakes than the manufacturer claims, but is delicious and devoid of the freeze-dried taste.

Pesto Green Basil Sauce. Imported from Italy and sometimes found in Italian groceries, this little can of basil, olive oil, and pecorino and Romano cheese is delicious when mixed with hot pasta and margarine.

Fritini Vegetable Patty mix. This product from Switzerland is frequently encountered in "health-food" stores and thus is quite expensive. Sahadi sells its Vegetable Burger Falafil Mix at a much more reasonable price.

Sökeland's Rye-Bread. You find this German product in "gourmet" stores that sell a lot of cheese, wine, bar tools, and fancy pepper mills. It's a tough little 8-ounce package of rye bread that keeps well and tastes delicious. Mestemacher has a 4-ounce packet of pumpernickel that is equally good.

And then there are *grits* again, for those of you who want something *really* exotic.

METRIC EQUIVALENT CHART

LIQUID VOLUME

1 fluid ounce (fl. oz)	=	30 milliliters (ml)
1 fluid cup (c)	=	240 milliliters (ml)
1 pint (pt)	=	470 milliliters (ml)
1 quart (qt)	=	950 milliliters (ml)
1 gallon (gal)	=	3.8 liters (l)
1 milliliter (ml)	=	.03 fluid ounces (fl. oz)
1 liter (l) or 1000 ml	=	2.1 fluid pints or 1.06 fluid quarts
1 liter (l)	=	.26 gallons (gal)

MASS WEIGHT

1 ounce (oz)	=	28 grams (g)
1 pound (lb)	=	450 grams (g)
1 gram (g)	=	.035 ounces (oz)
1 kilogram (kg) or 1000 g	=	2.2 pounds (lbs)

LENGTH

1 inch (in)	=	2.5 centimeters (cm)
1 foot (ft)	=	30 centimeters (cm)
1 millimeter (mm)	=	.04 inches (in)
1 centimeter (cm)	=	.4 inches (in)
1 meter (m)	=	3.3 feet (ft)

INDEX